FCE听力
从突破到跨越

（第二版）

（Ⅰ）

王宏 编著

中国人民大学出版社
·北京·

推荐序

FCE（First Certificate in English）是剑桥英语五级证书考试的第三级，通过五个模块来考查听、说、读、写四项能力。这项考试的难度相当于欧洲委员会指定的欧洲语言教学大纲的 B2 水平（中级学习者），即可以流利地表达自己，与母语人士进行交流并理解较为复杂的语言信息。FCE 考试不仅可以无缝对接雅思、托福等国际标准化考试，同时跟高考英语题型类似，因此很多同学和家长希望通过备考 FCE 考试来检验和提高英语水平。因此，本书除了可以有效帮助 FCE 考生在听力考试中取得好成绩，还适用于高考听口的训练以及托福听力的基础训练。

在 FCE 听力考试中，考生要具备捕捉信息以及准确理解细节的能力，因此一方面要熟悉词汇的发音，另一方面要能够灵活运用各种听力技巧，比如预测、推断等。本书采用了独特的训练方法，特别是用熟题做重听训练，可以让学生复盘理解信息在语境中的表达方式。这一方法在教学中取得了很好的效果。这次修订进一步强化了信息捕捉和理解训练。首先，尽管英语中有一些发音规则能够有效辅助一些单词的拼读，但是仍然需要学生进行拼写练习；此外，不同的场景中有一些特征词汇需要特别练习。因此，在这次修订过程中，增加了"分类补充词汇"。其次，英语中存在大量的同义词、近义词，在考试中形成题干和听力原文的对应关系，所以这次修订还专门增加了"近义词 & 同义词替换"。

王宏老师深耕基础英语教育二十余年，曾获得海淀区优秀教师奖励，熟知孩子学习的痛点、难点所在并积累了丰富的经验，制订了有效的解决方案。我自己的孩子在学习过程中也经常向她请教。她在担任剑桥五级考试考官期间，深入了解考试要点，建立了用考试促培训的教学体系，帮助数万名学生提升了能力并获得满意的成绩。

本书修订出版在即，谨以此文为序，愿更多的考生取得满意的成绩。

图书使用　　　图书使用　　　图书使用　　　图书使用
微信公众号　　微博　　　　　抖音号　　　　小红书号

更多图书使用资料，请扫码了解。

序

通过听带动说、读、写，是宏恩多年教学实践总结出的经验。本书以精听、听写为训练主题，话题直击真题，让学习更直接、更高效。听力一般不涉及生僻词，所用到的基本上是必须掌握的常用词汇。听力训练让学生学会地道的发音，有助于学生加强语法、词组搭配等方面的训练，也为口语和写作积累语料。

听力训练的过程，刚开始有点苦，但每一刻你都能感受到收获和进步。渐渐地，你会发现，音频里的语速越来越"慢"了，音频中人们说的话不再是混淆无序的，而是有结构的。同时，通过每日训练，你发现了自身的知识漏洞，也学到了非常具体的东西：单词、短语、语音、语法。

知识的海洋，任你遨游；梦想的天空，任你翱翔；人生的辉煌，等你开拓；英语的高分，等你挑战！

在本书的编写过程中，贾玉梅和北京美文苑文化发展有限公司参与了部分资料的收集和整理，在此一并表示感谢。

宏恩英语创始人

本书使用说明

本书内容以 FCE 听力题目为主。我们把每份听力题目的练习都分成三个步骤。首先，了解题目在考试中的出现形式和常考内容，按照考试要求完成，不暂停、不重播，然后对照答案自行批改；其次，重新播放音频，完成填空练习，这个过程中可以暂停，听不出的部分可以反复听；最后，对照填空内容看后面的听力原文，补全自己没听出来的部分或修改出错的部分，认真分析是因为发音问题，还是因为生词不会写，并多加朗读和模仿。精听训练需要不断按暂停键来填空，而不是 5 分钟的听力，5 分钟就填出来，有可能需要三个、四个、五个，甚至更多 5 分钟反复精听才能填上。磨耳朵的过程就是不断进步的过程，大家可以用红笔订正所填内容并朗读听力材料，坚持三个月后，就会有所收获。

欢迎关注宏恩英语微信公众号：Horn English，获取最新考试资讯，了解图书使用方法。

目 录
CONTENTS

CHAPTER 3   FCE LISTENING PART 3 /47

CHAPTER 4   FCE LISTENING PART 4 /63

FCE 听力原题答案 /85

CHAPTER 1 FCE LISTENING PART 1

FCE LISTENING

FCE LISTENING

FCE LISTENING

FCE LISTENING

FCE LISTENING

FCE LISTENING

FCE LISTENING

FCE LISTENING

FCE LISTENING

FCE LISTENING

FCE LISTENING

FCE LISTENING

SECTION 1

▶ 听力原题

Part 1

You will hear people talking in eight different situations. For Questions 1–8, choose the best answer (A, B or C).

1 You overhear a young man talking about his first job.

How did he feel in his first job?

A. annoyed

B. confused

C. enthusiastic

2 You hear a radio announcement about a dance company.

What are listeners being invited to?

A. a dancing show

B. a talk

C. a party

3 You overhear a woman talking to a man about something that happened to her.

Who was she?

A. a traveller

B. a driver

C. a passenger

4 You hear a woman talking on the radio about her work making wildlife films.

What is her main point?

A. Being in the right location at the right time is essential.

B. More time is spent planning than actually filming.

C. It is worthwhile spending time preparing.

5 You hear part of a travel programme on the radio.

Where is the speaker?

A. inside a white house

B. by the sea

C. on a lake

6　You overhear a woman talking about a table-tennis table in a sports shop.

What does she want the shop assistant to do about her table-tennis table?

A. give her a new table

B. have it put together for her

C. give her the money back

7　You hear part of an interview with a businesswoman.

What is her business?

A. hiring out boats

B. hiring out caravans

C. building fishing boats

8　You hear a man talking on the radio.

Who is talking?

A. an actor

B. a journalist

C. a viewer

▶ 填空练习

Question 1

I didn't want to __ _____ _____, so when I _____ school I went and got a job. My parents said if I was _____ _____ _____ they'd _____ _____ _____ _____, but if not I'd have to work. So I got a job in a big store, in the _____ _____…Actually, I think I had to go out and find out what I could do, because in school I wasn't _____ _____. So, when it came to _____ _____, I think I had to prove a lot of people wrong. So I really _____ _____ _____ _____… _____ _____ it was just selling socks in Harridges.

Question 2

The Hilton Dance Company have been at the Camden Theatre for almost a month now, _____ ____ ____ _____ _____ of mainly modern dances. The company _____ _____ _____ their twentieth year of _____ all over the world! But this week they'll ____ _____ ____ _____ from dancing, to give us an idea of how a dance company works. Top dancer and company manager Lisa West will be in the theatre, _____ _____ about the company's work, but all the dancers _____ ____ _____ too, so it's also your _____ _____ ____ _____! And, of course, you don't need to have _____ _____ of dance for this…

Question 3

Woman: I tell you, we _____ _____ _____! He _____ _____ _____ some _____ _____ if we _____ _____ so quickly.

Man: What did he do—just _____ _____ _____ without looking?

Woman: Yeah, Clare _____ something _____ _____ and I just _____ _____ ___ _____.

Man: Did he stop?

Woman: You're _____! Just _____ _____ _____ at us and _____ _____.

Man: And there was nobody behind you?

Woman: No, _____, _____ _____ _____ _____ _____ _____ _____.

Man: You were lucky. The road's always busy.

Question 4

The research for ___ _____ _____ _____ _____ can take up to a year, followed by about two year's filming, with four or five camera teams around the world _____ _____ _____ _____. Finding the right stories to film is only half the job. The other half is _____ ___ _____ _____ and then going out to help the camera-person film it. This can be difficult—you have to _____ _____ you're in the right place at the right time. So _____ _____ ___ _____. We spend a lot of time on the phone _____, getting advice from _____ _____.

Question 5

This is the most beautiful place I've _____ _____ and, believe me, in my _____ ___ __ _____ _____, I've seen some _____ _____. From the _____ of this small sailing boat, I have a wonderful view out over a _____ _____ ____ _____ blue water to the white houses of the village on the left, and then to the _____ _____ _____, which climb up to the _____ _____ _____ _____ this lovely valley. _____ ____ _____ _____, people are sitting in the _____ _____ _____ ___ _____ _____ of fresh fish, caught in these waters only a few hours ago. _____ _____!

Question 6

Giving me my money back _____ ___ _____. My son needs to _____ ___ ____ _____ _____, but _____ _____ _____ his table is _____ ____ _____ on the floor. When I bought it, I ____ _____ that it would only take __ _____ ___ ____ to _____ ____ _____ _____ ___ _____, but the instructions don't _____ _____. Since I paid so much for it, I think it's only fair to ask for some _____ _____ from you in getting it into ___ _____ _____. My son is _____ _____ a game on his new table!

Question 7

Interviewer: Helen, was this business always ___ _____ __ _____?

Woman: No, not really. It _____ from what we _____ _____ _____—build fishing boats.

Interviewer: How long _____ ___ _____ __ _____?

Woman: About eight years. First we built the _____, then we bought boats _____ _____ _____ ___ _____ _____. It's going well.

Interviewer: How many boats do you have? During the summer __ _____ _____ _____ _____.

Woman: Yes, people use them like _____, really. They go up river for their holidays and then bring them back to the moorings here for us to _____ _____ __ _____ _____…

Question 8

This is a _____ _____ _____—plenty to get your teeth into, some very _____ _____, a lot of change of mood. There's lots for ____ _____ ___ _____ _____ too, so it all goes to make my job _____ _____. The fact that this is a _____ _____ I also have the challenge of _____ ____ _____ _____ __ __ _____. The _____ _____, by the man who created the part some twenty years ago, will still be in the mind of some _____ _____ ___ _____. I couldn't ask for more.

▶ 听力原文

Question 1

I didn't want to go to university, so when I finished school I went and got a job. My parents said if I was in full-time education they'd give me an allowance, but if not I'd have to work. So I got a job in a big store, in the menswear department…Actually, I think I had to go out and find out what I could do, because in school I wasn't particularly brilliant. So, when it came to doing work, I think I had to prove a lot of people wrong. So I really felt like doing it…even though it was just selling socks in Harridges.

Question 2

The Hilton Dance Company have been at the Camden Theatre for almost a month now, offering us a wonderful programme of mainly modern dances. The company have just celebrated their twentieth year of performances all over the world! But this week they'll be taking a break from dancing, to give us an idea of how a dance company works. Top dancer and company manager Lisa West will be in the theatre, telling us about the company's work, but all the dancers will be there too, so it's also your opportunity for a get-together! And, of course, you don't need to have any experience of dance for this…

Question 3

Woman: I tell you, we were dead lucky! He could have done some serious damage if we hadn't reacted so quickly.

Man: What did he do—just shoot straight out without looking?

Woman: Yeah, Clare yelled something at me and I just slammed on the brakes.

Man: Did he stop?

Woman: You're joking! Just blasted his horn at us and carried on.

Man: And there was nobody behind you?

Woman: No, fortunately, otherwise who knows what might have happened.

Man: You were lucky. The road's always busy.

Question 4

The research for a major wildlife TV series can take up to a year, followed by about two year's filming, with four or five camera teams around the world at any one time. Finding the right stories to film is only half the job. The other half is finding the right location and then going out to help the camera-person film it. This can be difficult—you have to make sure you're in the right place at the right time. So good planning is essential. We spend a lot of time on the phone beforehand, getting advice from local experts.

Question 5

This is the most beautiful place I've ever visited and, believe me, in my career as a travel writer, I've seen some fabulous scenes. From the deck of this small sailing boat, I have a wonderful view out over a short expanse of sparkling blue water to the white houses of the village on the left, and then to the wooded hillsides behind, which climb up to the snow-covered mountain peaks surrounding this lovely valley. By the water's edge, people are sitting in the late-evening sun enjoying a leisurely meal of fresh fish, caught in these waters only a few hours ago. It's heaven!

Question 6

Giving me my money back isn't the point. My son needs to practise for an important match, but at the moment his table is lying in bits on the floor. When I bought it, I was assured that it would only take a matter of moments to screw the different parts in place, but the instructions don't make sense. Since I paid so much for it, I think it's only fair to ask for some hands-on help from you in getting it into a useable state. My son is impatient for a game on his new table!

Question 7

Interviewer: Helen, was this business always a dream of yours?

Woman: No, not really. It developed from what we used to do—build fishing boats.

Interviewer: How long have you been in business?

Woman: About eight years. First we built the marina, then we bought boats to rent out for cruising holidays. It's going well.

Interviewer: How many boats do you have? During the summer I bet you're pretty busy.

Woman: Yes, people use them like caravans, really. They go up river for their holidays and then bring them back to the moorings here for us to prepare for the next client…

Question 8

This is a really delicious part—plenty to get your teeth into, some very good speeches, a lot of change of mood. There's lots for the audience to identify with too, so it all goes to make my job more rewarding. The fact that this is a revival means I also have the challenge of putting my own stamp on a role. The original performance, by the man who created the part some twenty years ago, will still be in the mind of some members of the audience. I couldn't ask for more.

SECTION 2

▶ 听力原题

Part 1

You will hear people talking in eight different situations. For Questions 1–8, choose the best answer (A, B or C).

---

1   You hear part of an interview in which a film director talks about his favourite movie.

    Why does he like the film?

    A. It is very funny.

    B. It is very exciting.

    C. It is very educational.

2   You hear a man talking about a sofa he bought.

    What is he complaining about?

    A. He received the wrong sofa.

    B. He was required to double pay the sofa.

    C. The sofa was damaged.

3   You hear an actor talking about using different accents in his work.

    What point is he making about actors?

    A. They need to acquire standard English.

    B. They have to be able to control their use of accents.

    C. They should try to keep their original accents.

4   You hear part of an interview in which a man is talking about winning his first horse race.

    What does he say about it?

    A. He found it rather disappointing.

    B. He didn't have a chance to celebrate.

    C. He has no energy to care.

5   You hear a writer of musicals talking on the radio.

    What is he trying to explain?

    A. why his aunt's career was not very successful

    B. the relationship between American and British musicals

    C. his reasons for becoming a writer of musicals

6   You hear the beginning of a lecture about ancient history.

    What is the lecture going to be about?

    A. trade in arms and weapons

    B. trade in decorative goods

    C. trade in works of art

7   You hear a man talking about travelling from London to France for his job.

    What does he say about the train journey?

    A. He's able to use it to his advantage.

    B. It is a no mobile phone workplace.

    C. He enjoys the social aspect of it.

8   You hear a woman in a shop talking about some lost photographs.

    What does she think the shop should give her?

    A. some money

    B. a role of new film

    C. an apology

▶ 填空练习

Question 1

Interviewer: So, do you have a favourite movie?

Director: Oh…that's difficult. Well, I think it ____ ___ ___ *The Agents*, the Mel Rivers movie. I like it because it _____ ____ that ____ _____ _____ ____ _____ ____, or how many times you ____ _____ _____ by bad situations, things can get ___ _____ ____ ____.

Interviewer: When did you first see it?

Director: On television, late one night…I _____ _____ _____ about sixteen. There were moments when I just _____ ____ _____. It's _____ ____ _____, but it's very warm. I love the friendship that _____ _____ ____ ____ _____ _____.

Question 2

I think this is the last time I'm buying anything from that shop. I can't believe ____ _____ _____ _____! But they've got _____ _____. The next time I buy a sofa, I'd ___ _____ ___ _____ double to _____ ___ ___ _____. They came to _____ ___, and when I saw it I thought, 'This isn't the sofa I chose, maybe the colour looks different ____ _____.' But it was mine. And then I realised that _____ ___ ___ _____ at the back _____ _____ and ___ _____ was coming out. So I got them to _____ ___ _____ and now I have to wait two weeks to _____ ___ _____.

Question 3

Most actors start out with __ ____ ___ __ _____ or _____ _____ of some sort, but what _____ ___ _____ is that, at drama school, _____ ___ ___ _____ is to acquire what's called 'standard English'. So you lose your original accent and when somebody says, you know, 'Do something in your old voice, it takes __ _____ ___ _____ to click in and ____ _____ _____ _____ it again, I phone my parents and they say, 'My, you sound so English!' but then over here I sometimes don't get work because people can hear that I'm actually Australian, so I've got ___ _____ _____ work to do there.

Question 4

Interviewer: Can you still _____ ___ _____ ____ it? I mean, the first time you actually ride out there, out in front must be…

Man: Yeah, yeah, it was certainly __ _____ _____, but it was an evening event. It was the last race and it was almost dark by the time we'd finished and when I got home it was about ten or eleven o'clock, so there was very little time to _____ _____ ___ or do anything. And I _____ ___ ___ ____ at about half five the next day for my job, so _____ it was _____ _____ ___ _____ really.

Question 5

I ___ _____ _____ ____ the musical theatre, from the very word go. My aunt was an actress, ___ __ _____ _____ _____, but I thought her world was _____ _____. And she used to take me to London to see some of the American musicals which were on in Great Britain some time after they were on in New York, and so I got to see a lot of things at a very early age. It just _____ ___; it was _____ ___ _____ _____.

Question 6

The _____ _____ ___ _____ _____ go back to the Ancient Greek period, with _____ _____ _____ ___ _____ _____. Unlike the trade in _____ _____ ___ _____ _____, however, few written records remain. So we _____ ____ _____ _____, which does show, for example, that _____ _____ _____ spread from Greece to the rest of Europe. And using the type of research _____ _____ _____ _____ ___ _____ ___ _____ _____, we can now show how the equipment necessary to do battle _____ _____ _____.

Question 7

The best thing about the Eurostar train is that it is city centre to city centre. I almost always _____ _____ and we use the train as a second office. Sometimes there are ____ _____ ___ ____ ____ ____ and I _____ _____ _____ to have on the train. I _____ _____ and _____ who have meetings in Paris on the same day to travel with us so we can _____ _____. It's __ _____ _____ to talk _____ ___ _____ of the office—we don't _____ ___ _____ _____ _____.

Question 8

It's ___ _____ ___ _____ _____ saying you're sorry, because that isn't going to give me the photographs you've lost, is it? And I took them on a _____ _____, so it's _____ ___ _____ them. It didn't _____ ____ _____ for an instant that you could _____ __ _____ ___ _____, just like that. ____ _____ _____, I think it's ___ _____ just to offer me a new roll in its place. I _____ _____ at the very least to ___ _____ ___ _____, and _____ ___ ___ _____ and _____, even if it isn't your _____ _____.

▶ 听力原文

Question 1

Interviewer: So, do you have a favourite movie?

Director: Oh…that's difficult. Well, I think it has to be *The Agents*, the Mel Rivers movie. I like it because it reminds you that no matter how hard life is, or how many times you get knocked down by bad situations, things can get a whole lot worse.

Interviewer: When did you first see it?

Director: On television, late one night…I must have been about sixteen. There were moments when I just couldn't stop laughing. It's anarchic and silly, but it's very warm. I love the friendship that develops between the two main characters.

Question 2

I think this is the last time I'm buying anything from that shop. I can't believe how inefficient they are! But they've got reasonable prices. The next time I buy a sofa, I'd be prepared to pay double to avoid all this stress. They came to deliver it, and when I saw it I thought, 'This isn't the sofa I chose, maybe the colour looks different in daylight.' But it was mine. And then I realised that part of the cover at the back was torn and the filling was coming out. So I got them to take it away and now I have to wait two weeks to get it replaced.

Question 3

Most actors start out with a bit of a regional or non-standard accent of some sort, but what tends to happen is that, at drama school, part of the training is to acquire what's called 'standard English'. So you lose your original accent and when somebody says, you know, 'Do something in your old voice,' it takes a couple of minutes to click in and get your head round it again. I phone my parents and they say, 'My, you sound so English!' but then over here I sometimes don't get work because people can hear that I'm actually Australian, so I've got a bit more work to do there.

Question 4

Interviewer: Can you still remember the thrill of it? I mean, the first time you actually ride out there, out in front must be…

Man: Yeah, yeah, it was certainly a big thrill, but it was an evening event. It was the last race and it was almost dark by the time we'd finished and when I got home it was about ten or eleven o'clock, so there was very little time to think about it or do anything. And I had to be up at about half five the next day for my job, so unfortunately it was straight back to work really.

Question 5

I was always fascinated by the musical theatre, from the very word go. My aunt was an actress, not a particularly successful one, but I thought her world was unbelievably glamorous. And she used to take me to London to see some of the American musicals which were on in Great Britain some time after they were on in New York, and so I got to see a lot of things at a very early age. It just grabbed me; it was one of those things.

Question 6

The earliest records of this trade go back to the Ancient Greek period, with various deals around the Mediterranean area. Unlike the trade in more decorative or luxury goods, however, few written records remain. So we mostly rely on archaeological evidence, which does show, for example, that designs for swords spread from Greece to the rest of Europe. And using the type of research more usually associated with the spread of artistic trends, we can now show how the equipment necessary to do battle was being exported.

Question 7

The best thing about the Eurostar train is that it is city centre to city centre. I almost always travel with colleagues and we use the train as a second office. Sometimes there are as many as nine of us and I schedule formal meetings to have on the train. I invite suppliers and clients who have meetings in Paris on the same day to travel with us so we can discuss business. It's a perfect opportunity to talk without the distractions of the office—we don't switch on our mobile phones.

Question 8

It's no good just standing there saying you're sorry, because that isn't going to give me the photographs you've lost, is it? And I took them on a once-in-a-lifetime holiday, so it's impossible to replace them. It didn't cross my mind for an instant that you could lose a roll of film, just like that. To be frank, I think it's an insult just to offer me a new roll in its place. I would expect at the very least to be offered a refund, and compensation for the loss and inconvenience, even if it isn't your normal policy.

SECTION 3

▶ 听力原题

Part 1

You will hear people talking in eight different situations. For Questions 1–8, choose the best answer (A, B or C).

---

1 You hear a man talking to a group of people who are going on an expedition into the rainforest.

What does he advise them against?

A. camping overnight by the river

B. using substances which attract insects

C. bathing in areas where insects are common

2 You overhear two people talking about a school football competition.

What did the woman think of the event?

A. It was boring because not many teams showed up.

B. It managed to fulfil its aims.

C. Not enough people had helped to set it up.

3 You hear a woman talking about her studies at the Beijing Opera School.

How did she feel when she first started her classes?

A. anxious about being the oldest student in her class

B. disappointed because her dictionary was unhelpful

C. annoyed by the lack of communication with her teacher

4 You hear a famous comedian talking on the radio about his early career.

Why is he telling this story?

A. to show how lucky he was at the beginning

B. to show the importance of work experiences

C. to show that he has always been a good comedian

5 You hear someone talking on the phone.

Who is she talking to?

A. someone at her office

B. a ticket agent

C. a family member

6　You hear a novelist talking about how she writes.

How does she get her ideas for her novels?

A. She bases her novels on travelling experiences.

B. Ideas come to her once she starts writing.

C. She lets ideas develop gradually in her mind.

7　You hear a woman talking to a friend on the phone.

What is she doing?

A. accepting an invitation

B. denying an accusation

C. apologising for a mistake

8　You hear a radio announcement about a future programme.

What kind of programme is it?

A. a play about a child

B. a story about family lives

C. a holiday programme

▶ 填空练习

Question 1

Because you need water for ＿＿＿＿ ＿＿＿＿, you often ＿＿＿ ＿＿＿ ＿＿＿ ＿＿＿ ＿＿＿ ＿＿＿ by a river. ＿＿＿＿＿ ＿＿ ＿＿ ＿＿＿ to keep insects away, this can be ＿＿ ＿＿＿＿ ＿＿ ＿＿＿ ＿＿ ＿＿. Much as you might feel you need a good wash, one trap not to fall into, though, is the use of soap or shampoo. These may make you feel good, but actually ＿＿＿ ＿＿ ＿＿＿＿＿ ＿＿＿ in the jungle which act as a ＿＿＿＿＿ ＿＿ ＿＿＿, thus ＿＿＿＿＿＿ ＿＿ ＿＿＿＿ ＿＿ ＿＿ ＿＿＿＿ ＿＿＿. Better to actually go in for a dip, ＿＿＿＿ ＿＿＿＿＿ ＿＿ ＿＿ ＿＿ and ＿＿＿ ＿＿ ＿＿＿＿ ＿＿ ＿＿ ＿＿ ＿＿＿.

Question 2

Man:　So, how did the school football competition go on Saturday? Sorry I didn't ＿＿＿ ＿＿ ＿＿ ＿＿＿, but I had so much to do, you know how it is.

Woman:　Oh, don't worry—luckily some of the other parents ＿＿＿ ＿＿＿ ＿＿ ＿＿＿. We just didn't ＿＿＿ ＿＿ ＿＿＿ ＿＿＿ ＿＿ ＿＿ ＿＿＿ ＿＿ ＿＿＿, and I thought the whole thing ＿＿＿ ＿＿ ＿＿＿＿ ＿＿ ＿＿ ＿＿＿. You know, of course, ＿＿ ＿＿ ＿＿ ＿＿ ＿＿ raise some money to ＿＿＿ ＿＿＿ new trees in the school grounds. Well, we ＿＿＿＿ ＿＿＿, and my kids thought the whole afternoon was great, so I guess it was OK.

Question 3

I was twenty-four when I went to China and _____ the Beijing Opera School to _____ ___ _____ as their first _____ _____. I was _____ ____ _____ of the other students and _____ _____ _____ _____. At the interview I arrived with my little Chinese-English _____, which was quite funny, as it helped _____ _____ them, 'cause they thought: This girl is __ _____. When I actually started the lessons it was very _____ both for me and my teacher. Most of the time we were _____ _____ at each other and _____. I just had to _____ ___ _____ ____ _____ _____. I learnt the _____ ____ _____ through that school…

Question 4

___ _____ _____, I sort of _____ ____ _____ _____. I was doing this course in media studies, which meant, you know, looking at cameras and drinking lots of coffee. And one day, we visited a television station as, like, _____ _____. And they were making this _____ _____ and said they were _____ _____ a new comedian because someone had _____ ____ _____, and so myself and my friend _____. It's still __ _____ to me why, but they liked us, and so I was on _____ _____ ____ ____ _____ ____ about seventeen. We thought we were _____ _____, but I'm glad to say ___ _____ _____ of those programmes.

Question 5

So tell me again, what time does that train _____ ____? I see. That's a bit late, because I wouldn't really have enough time to get from the station to my meeting. _____ _____ the one before that, what time does that one arrive? Yes, that sounds better. __ ____ _____ ____ _____? Will you see to that for me and leave the tickets on my desk? No, __ _____ _____, I'll be at my mother's for the weekend. Can you post them to me there? It'll save time all round. Thanks.

Question 6

I get lots of ideas for novels, but I don't _____ _____ _____ ___ ____. Only when they _____ _____ over a period of years ____ ___ _____ that a particular idea ____ ____ ____ ___ _____ ____ ____. That's certainly what happened with my _____ _____, *The Red Cord*. Although _____ ____ ____ my home city of Sydney, Australia, ___ _____ ___ ___ _____ came about ten years ago when I was travelling in China. This ____ _____ ___ a long period when the idea _____ ____ ____ ___ ____ _____, each time _____ ___ _____ _____, until I _____ __ _____ where I thought I'd better start writing.

Question 7

What do you mean, Mary, when you say I never _____ _____ _____ ___ _____ _____? No, sorry. I can't _____ _____. I invited everybody round here for a party on my last birthday, remember? I was going to _____ _____ _____ _____ _____ all and then Henry and Mark _____ ____ _____ us out to that new Japanese restaurant in town. It's true that I _____ _____ _____, but I thought it _____ ____ _____ _____ _____ _____.

Question 8

_____ of long summer days ____ ___ _____ are recalled in *The Last Summer*, our family drama this afternoon. The Finnish children's writer Tove Jansson, well known for her stories about family life, wrote *The Last Summer*, __ _____ _____ of her own long _____ summers spent on an _____ _____ with her grandmother. There are _____ _____ by Moira Harmer and Alice Williams. Tune in to *The Last Summer* at two o'clock this afternoon and ___ _____ to an island in a blue sea, far away from the world of work.

▶ 听力原文

Question 1

Because you need water for various reasons, you often end up making your overnight camp by a river. Providing you take care to keep insects away, this can be as healthy a place as any. Much as you might feel you need a good wash, one trap not to fall into, though, is the use of soap or shampoo. These may make you feel good, but actually give off unnatural smells in the jungle which act as a magnet to insects, thus increasing the chances of your getting bitten. Better to actually go in for a dip, being careful to dry off and re-apply your anti-insect cream immediately afterwards.

Question 2

Man: So, how did the school football competition go on Saturday? Sorry I didn't turn up to help, but I had so much to do, you know how it is.

Woman: Oh, don't worry—luckily some of the other parents came along to help. We just didn't attract as many teams as we thought we would, and I thought the whole thing lacked any excitement as a result. You know, of course, that the point was to raise some money to pay for new trees in the school grounds. Well, we achieved that, and my kids thought the whole afternoon was great, so I guess it was OK.

Question 3

I was twenty-four when I went to China and persuaded the Beijing Opera School to take me on as their first western pupil. I was twice the age of the other students and hardly spoke their language. At the interview I arrived with my little Chinese-English dictionary, which was quite funny, as it helped towards persuading them, 'cause they thought: This girl is so determined. When I actually started the lessons it was very irritating both for me and my teacher. Most of the time we were making signs at each other and misunderstanding. I just had to remain as patient as they were. I learnt the lesson of patience through that school…

Question 4

To be honest, I sort of fell on my feet. I was doing this course in media studies, which meant, you know, looking at cameras and drinking lots of coffee. And one day, we visited a television station as, like, work experience. And they were making this variety show and said they were looking for a new comedian because someone had let them down, and so myself and my friend volunteered. It's still a mystery to me why, but they liked us, and so I was on live television at the age of about seventeen. We thought we were absolutely brilliant, but I'm glad to say no copy exists of those programmes.

Question 5

So tell me again, what time does that train get in? I see. That's a bit late, because I wouldn't really have enough time to get from the station to my meeting. What about the one before that, what time does that one arrive? Yes, that sounds better. Is it necessary to book? Will you see to that for me and leave the tickets on my desk? No, on second thoughts, I'll be at my mother's for the weekend. Can you post them to me there? It'll save time all round. Thanks.

Question 6

I get lots of ideas for novels, but I don't necessarily follow them all up. Only when they stick around over a period of years do I realise that a particular idea has really got a hold on me. That's certainly what happened with my latest novel, *The Red Cord*. Although it's set in my home city of Sydney, Australia, the stirrings of an idea came about ten years ago when I was travelling in China. This was followed by a long period when the idea occasionally came back into my consciousness, each time refined a little more, until I reached a point where I thought I'd better start writing.

Question 7

What do you mean, Mary, when you say I never invite friends round to my house? No, sorry. I can't accept that. I invited everybody round here for a party on my last birthday, remember? I was going to cook something special for you all and then Henry and Mark insisted on taking us out to that new Japanese restaurant in town. It's true that I accepted their offer, but I thought it would be very rude to refuse.

Question 8

Memories of long summer days by the sea are recalled in *The Last Summer*, our family drama this afternoon. The Finnish children's writer Tove Jansson, well known for her stories about family life, wrote *The Last Summer*, a magical recreation of her own long childhood summers spent on an isolated island with her grandmother. There are superb performances by Moira Harmer and Alice Williams. Tune in to *The Last Summer* at two o'clock this afternoon and be transported to an island in a blue sea, far away from the world of work.

SECTION 4

▶ 听力原题

Part 1

You will hear people talking in eight different situations. For Questions 1–8, choose the best answer (A, B or C).

---

1   On a train, you overhear a woman phoning her office.

    Why has she phoned?

    A. to check the time of an appointment

    B. to apologise for losing her diary

    C. to find out where her diary is

2   You switch on the radio in the middle of a programme.

    What kind of programme is it?

    A. a nature programme

    B. a cookery programme

    C. a safety programme

3   You overhear a conversation between a watchmaker and a customer.

    What does the watchmaker say about the watch?

    A. It is impossible to repair it.

    B. It is not worth repairing.

    C. He has to pay for the new parts.

4   You overhear a woman talking about her new neighbours.

    How does she feel?

    A. offended

    B. admiring

    C. suspicious

5   You hear a man talking about deep-sea diving.

    Why does he like the sport?

    A. He has conflicts with his wife.

    B. It contrasts with his normal lifestyle.

    C. It fulfils his need for a challenge in life.

6   You turn on the radio and hear a scientist being interviewed about violins.

What is the scientist doing?

A. explaining how a violin works

B. explaining how a violin is made

C. explaining what makes a violin valuable

7   You hear part of a radio programme about CD-ROMs.

What is the speaker's opinion of the CD-ROMs about Australia which she tried?

A. Most of them are disappointing.

B. You are better off with an ordinary guidebook.

C. Most of them provide information by a single-page pictorial index.

8   You turn on the radio and hear a woman giving advice to business people.

What advice does she give about dealing with customers?

A. Force them not to call again.

B. Don't be too sympathetic towards them.

C. Don't allow them to stay on the phone too long.

▶ 填空练习

Question 1

Jenny, hi, it's me. I'm on the train and it's _____ _____ just outside the station—_____ _____ ___ _____…Yes, I know, sorry, but there's nothing I can do about it. Anyway, listen, could you _____ ___ _____ and see when I'm _____ ___ ____ _____ _____ _____? …It's on my desk…Oh, isn't it? Oh, that's strange. And it's not __ ___ _____? I wonder…Oh, I know, I _____ _____ _____ it in Jimmie's office after yesterday's meeting. You couldn't get it and then ring me back, could you? Sorry to be __ _____. Thanks a lot.

Question 2

Eggs are delicious food and parents have to _____ _____ they ____ _____ ___ _____ well _____ ____ _____ _____. One such careful parent _____ ___ _____ ___ _____ ___ of the Iguacu waterfalls in _____ _____ to _____ ___ _____ __ ___ _____ _____ in the rock face behind the falling water. _____ ___ _____, but _____ __ _____ is _____ _____. ____ _____ _____, there are no eggs on the menu in this particular part of South America, which is bad news for some!

Question 3

Customer: There's something wrong with my watch. It's running slow.

Woman: Oh, a Lexor. It's a common problem with the older Lexor watches. The _____ ____ are much better!

Customer: That's no help to me.

Woman: No, I _____ not. Anyway. It's not easy to _____ _____ _____, _____. Not many people are _____ ___ ____.

Customer: Right. So…?

Woman: And the problem is that by the time you've _____ __ __ _____ and put in the new parts and _____ it, you might as well _____ _____ it. It's always the same, and it's just as _____ __ ___ _____ _____ __ __ _____ __ _____.

Question 4

I must say, it surprised me when I saw how many there were in the family. I don't see how they're all going to ____ __ ____ _____ _____. And they're obviously quite _____—you _____ _____ _____ ____ _____ ___ _____ _____ that was carried in, and they've got three large cars between them—so why would a _____ _____ like that want to live here? It makes you wonder how they ____ _____ _____. Not that I've got anything to _____ _____—they've been _____ _____ _____ I've spoken to any of them, though so far they haven't found time to come in for a coffee.

Question 5

I love _____ _____. I go at least once every summer. _____ _____ _____ ___, the _____ _____ _____, until finally all you can hear is the sound of your own _____. It's my way of _____ _____ _____ ___ ____, finding some peace for once. I _____ my honeymoon _____, although my wife's not so _____, and it's not something we always do together. I don't ____ _____ _____, and I'm not _____ ____ _____ _____. I did, however, once join some guys in a cage off Florida, _____ ____ ___ _____ _____ _____. If sharks stop moving, they die. That sounds like me back home!

Question 6

Interviewer: It's difficult to talk about ____ _____ ___ ___ _____, but our great musicians today still clearly feel that these sixteenth-century _____ _____ are the best. Do you agree with them?

Scientist: Well, if you _____ _____ ____ a violin, um…it may be a _____ _____, but it is _____ ____ ___ _____ ____, _____ _____ is to take a little energy ____ ____ ___ _____ that the musician plays and to turn it into sound that ___ _____ _____ by the listener. The function of an individual violin is to _____ _____ _____ and sound qualities for the musician to _____ ___ ___ ___ _____ _____.

Question 7

If, like me, you're about to _____ _____ ___ _____ and you haven't yet bought a _____, how about trying a CD-ROM instead? Be careful though, ____ _____ _____ interactive CDs turn out to be a _____. Many _____ _____ _____ _____ ___ _____ _____, add a few _____ _____ and expect the buying public to be _____. I wasn't. In this _____, Wilson's _____ _____ is a _____ _____. It's got all the information, _____ _____ from a single-page _____ ____ _____ _____, cities, wildlife, famous people, etc., and the _____ __ _____ __ good still pictures and ninety-two _____ _____.

Question 8

If you have to _____ _____ __ _____ who _____ _____ your office about a problem you think you've already dealt with, it's important to be _____. Make them understand that you really _____ ____ _____ _____, but decide on a course of action early in the conversation and try to _____ ____ _____ quickly to _____ ____ _____ _____. If you can, it _____ ___ _____ your while trying to discover if there is another reason for their _____, to try to do something about it before they call again.

▶ 听力原文

Question 1

Jenny, hi, it's me. I'm on the train and it's stuck somewhere just outside the station—signalling problems or something…Yes, I know, sorry, but there's nothing I can do about it. Anyway, listen, could you check my diary and see when I'm supposed to be with those marketing people? …It's on my desk…Oh, isn't it? Oh, that's strange. And it's not in the drawer? I wonder…Oh, I know, I must have left it in Jimmie's office after yesterday's meeting. You couldn't get it and then ring me back, could you? Sorry to be a nuisance. Thanks a lot.

Question 2

Eggs are delicious food and parents have to make sure they are laid in spots well hidden from hungry thieves. One such careful parent braves the rushing waters of the Iguacu waterfalls in South America to lay its eggs in a damp crack in the rock face behind the falling water. Accidents are frequent, but evidently the risk is considered worthwhile. In any case, there are no eggs on the menu in this particular part of South America, which is bad news for some!

Question 3

Customer: There's something wrong with my watch. It's running slow.

Woman: Oh, a Lexor. It's a common problem with the older Lexor watches. The latest ones are much better!

Customer: That's no help to me.

Woman: No, I suppose not. Anyway. It's not easy to get them fixed, either. Not many people are up to it.

Customer: Right. So…?

Woman: And the problem is that by the time you've got it to pieces and put in the new parts and reassembled it, you might as well have replaced it. It's always the same, and it's just as likely to go wrong again in a couple of months.

Question 4

I must say, it surprised me when I saw how many there were in the family. I don't see how they're all going to fit in that small house. And they're obviously quite well-off—you should have seen the amounts of electronic equipment that was carried in, and they've got three large cars between them—so why would a wealthy family like that want to live here? It makes you wonder how they earn their living. Not that I've got anything to complain about—they've been perfectly pleasant whenever I've spoken to any of them, though so far they haven't found time to come in for a coffee.

Question 5

I love deep-sea diving. I go at least once every summer. The deeper you go, the quieter everything becomes, until finally all you can hear is the sound of your own heartbeat. It's my way of getting away from it all, finding some peace for once. I spent my honeymoon diving, although my wife's not so keen, and it's not something we always do together. I don't need company necessarily, and I'm not looking for some incredible adventure. I did, however, once join some guys in a cage off Florida, searching for the great white shark. If sharks stop moving, they die. That sounds like me back home!

Question 6

Interviewer: It's difficult to talk about the beauty of a sound, but our great musicians today still clearly feel that these sixteenth-century Italian violins are the best. Do you agree with them?

Scientist: Well, if you look closely at a violin, um…it may be a beautiful-looking instrument, but it is basically just a wooden box, whose function is to take a little energy out of the string that the musician plays and to turn it into sound that is then heard by the listener. The function of an individual violin is to provide suitable playing and sound qualities for the musician to express all of his or her emotions.

Question 7

If, like me, you're about to set off for Australia and you haven't yet bought a guidebook, how about trying a CD-ROM instead? Be careful though, the majority of interactive CDs turn out to be a let-down. Many publishers convert printed material to digital format, add a few flashy linkages and expect the buying public to be impressed. I wasn't. In this context, Wilson's multimedia package is a refreshing contrast. It's got all the information, readily accessed from a single-page pictorial index covering states, cities, wildlife, famous people, etc., and the data is accompanied by good still pictures and ninety-two video clips.

Question 8

If you have to deal with a customer who keeps ringing your office about a problem you think you've already dealt with, it's important to be forceful. Make them understand that you really sympathise with their problem, but decide on a course of action early in the conversation and try to keep it moving quickly to avoid any difficult areas. If you can, it might be worth your while trying to discover if there is another reason for their persistence, to try to do something about it before they call again.

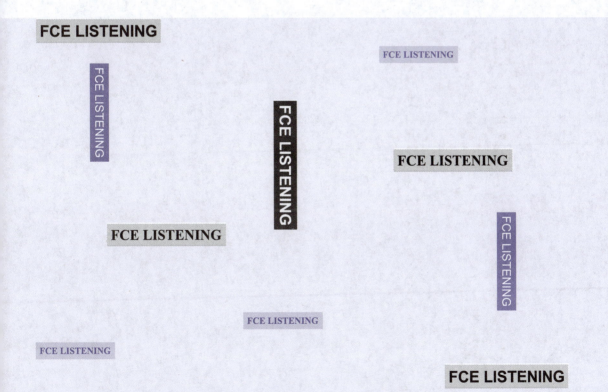

SECTION 1

▶ 听力原题

Part 2

You will hear a radio interview with Mike Reynolds, whose hobby is exploring underground places such as caves. For Questions 9–18, complete the sentences.

Cavers explore underground places such as mines and [_____ 9_____] as well as caves.

When cavers camp underground, they choose places which have [_____ and _____ 10] available.

In the UK. the place Mike likes best for caving is [_____ 11_____].

As a physical activity, Mike compares caving to [_____ 12_____].

Cavers can pay as much as £20 for a suitable [_____ 13_____].

Cavers can pay as much as £50 for the right kind of [_____ 14_____], which is worn on the head.

Mike recommends buying expensive [_____ 15_____] to avoid having accidents.

Caving is a sport for people of [_____ 16_____] and backgrounds.

Some caves in Britain are called places of [_____ 17_____].

The need for safety explains why people don't organise caving [_____ 18_____].

▶ 填空练习

Interviewer: In the studio with me today I have Mike Reynolds, who's what ____ _____ ___ ___ _____. In other words, he _____ long periods of time _____ _____ _____ ____ _____. And Mike's here to tell us all about this _____ _____ and how to get started on it. So Mike, why caves?

Mike: Well, cavers actually explore any space _____ _____, whether it's caves, ____ _____ __ _____.

Interviewer: Oh, right. So how big are these underground spaces?

Mike: Oh, anything up to eighty kilometres long…which means that, in some cases, ____ _____ ___ _____ ___ _____, you've got to sleep, to _____ _____ _____, inside the cave at some point—usually where both space and fresh air ___ _____.

Interviewer: No good if you're _____ ____ ___ _____.

Mike: No.

Interviewer: So where do you find the best caves?

Mike: ___ _____ ____ _____, the best places are, for example, _____, _____ and ____ _____. Here in the UK, various areas have the right _____ ___ _____. My favourite is Wales, but you can find plenty of caves in northern England and in Scotland too.

Interviewer: _____ _____ ___ ____ __ _____ _____, doesn't it?

Mike: That's right…in terms of _____ _____, it's very _____ ___ _____ except they go up and we go down. The _____ can be very different though…We often find ourselves _____ _____ ____ _____ in the rock, which we have to _____ _____ __ __ _____ ___ _____.

Interviewer: So the right _____ ___ _____ _____ _____. If I wanted to _____ _____ ____ __ _____ like this, what would I need?

Mike: Well, you'd need a _____ ____, and it's important to get one that ___ _____, so that it doesn't _____ _____ over your eyes or feel _____ _____, and these can cost anything from five to twenty pounds.

Interviewer: Umm…that doesn't _____ ____ _____ ____ _____.

Mike: Oh but then there's the lamp. You wear that on your head because it's very important to _____ _____ _____ _____ at all times. But it doesn't come with the hat and it can _____ _____ ____ ____ fifty pounds to get a _____ one.

Interviewer: I guess warm clothes are ___ _____ too?

Mike: You'll need to spend thirty to forty pounds on a _____ ____ because the caves can be _____ ___ and cold inside and you can get ill if you're ___ _____. Then, of course, the thing that you really need to spend money on is something for your feet that _____ __ _____ _____. Strong boots are _____ ___ _____, also because without them you could ___ _____ ___ ___ _____ and _____ _____ ___ _____. Cheap ones are just not as safe. I'm afraid.

Interviewer: It sounds pretty _____. I mean, is it really only a sport for the young and fit?

Mike: That's quite interesting, because people _____ ___ _____ that, but in fact cavers come _____ ___ _____ and _____—students and professionals alike. You even find eight-year-olds who've been doing it for years.

Interviewer: What exactly is it that people find so _____?

Mike: It's _____…the _____ ___ _____ ____ finding something new—a passage that nobody knew about before or a piece of rock that's just lovely to look at.

Interviewer: And I understand that _____ _____ _____ _____ __ ____ _____ ___ _____.

Mike: Yes. Forty-eight caves in Britain _____ ____ _____ _____ '_____ ___ _____ _____' because of what they _____, and this is the same in other countries too.

Interviewer: So, do cavers enjoy _____, like in other sports?

Mike: No. We want to enjoy a safe sport and, ____ _____ ___ _____ that, there are __ _____ ____ _____. We try to _____ ___ _____ ___ _____, but the _____ is on _____ and the _____ of the sport for what it can _____ ___ _____.

Interviewer: Well, it sounds like something I'll have to try one day. Mike, thank you very much for coming in and sharing…

▶ 听力原文

Interviewer: In the studio with me today I have Mike Reynolds, who's what is known as a caver. In other words, he spends long periods of time exploring underground caves for pleasure. And Mike's here to tell us all about this fascinating hobby and how to get started on it. So Mike, why caves?

Mike: Well, cavers actually explore any space that's underground, whether it's caves, old mines or tunnels.

Interviewer: Oh, right. So how big are these underground spaces?

Mike: Oh, anything up to eighty kilometres long…which means that, in some cases, in order to reach the end, you've got to sleep, to set up camp, inside the cave at some point—usually where both space and fresh air are available.

Interviewer: No good if you're afraid of the dark.

Mike: No.

Interviewer: So where do you find the best caves?

Mike: In terms of countries, the best places are, for example, Ireland, Australia and the Philippines. Here in the UK, various areas have the right sort of geology. My favourite is Wales, but you can find plenty of caves in northern England and in Scotland too.

Interviewer: Caving involves a lot of physical exercises, doesn't it?

Mike: That's right…in terms of physical activity, it's very similar to climbing except they go up and we go down. The conditions can be very different though…We often find ourselves facing very small gaps in the rock, which we have to crawl through on our hands and knees.

Interviewer: So the right equipment is obviously very important. If I wanted to start out on a hobby like this, what would I need?

Mike: Well, you'd need a hard hat, and it's important to get one that fits properly, so that it doesn't keep falling over your eyes or feel too tight, and these can cost anything from five to twenty pounds.

Interviewer: Umm… that doesn't sound too much for starters.

Mike: Oh but then there's the lamp. You wear that on your head because it's very important to keep your hands free at all times. But it doesn't come with the hat and it can cost anything up to fifty pounds to get a suitable one.

Interviewer: I guess warm clothes are a must too?

Mike: You'll need to spend thirty to forty pounds on a waterproof suit because the caves can be pretty wet and cold inside and you can get ill if you're not protected. Then, of course, the thing that you really need to spend money on is something for your feet that keeps the water out. Strong boots are essential for this, also because without them you could be slipping on wet surfaces and doing yourself an injury. Cheap ones are just not as safe. I'm afraid.

Interviewer: It sounds pretty tough. I mean, is it really only a sport for the young and fit?

Mike: That's quite interesting, because people tend to think that, but in fact cavers come from all ages and backgrounds—students and professionals alike. You even find eight-year-olds who've been doing it for years.

Interviewer: What exactly is it that people find so attractive?

Mike: It's excitement…the pleasure you get in finding something new—a passage that nobody knew about before or a piece of rock that's just lovely to look at.

Interviewer: And I understand that conservation has become a key issue as well.

Mike: Yes. Forty-eight caves in Britain are now known as 'places of special interest' because of what they contain, and this is the same in other countries too.

Interviewer: So, do cavers enjoy competing, like in other sports?

Mike: No. We want to enjoy a safe sport and, in order to ensure that, there are no competitions in caving. We try to organise a range of events, but the emphasis is on co-operation and the enjoyment of the sport for what it can offer the individual.

Interviewer: Well, it sounds like something I'll have to try one day. Mike, thank you very much for coming in and sharing…

SECTION 2

▶ 听力原题

Part 2

You will hear part of a radio interview with a woman who sailed round the world on her own. For Questions 9–18, complete the sentences.

Anna was employed by a [　　9　　] when she first started sailing.

The idea of sailing round the world came from a book called [　　10].

Anna spent some time [　　11] the boat before taking it out to sea.

Anna tested her boat on a trip which lasted for only [　　12] because it was damaged.

Anna got the money she needed to make the trip from various [　　13] companies.

Anna's worst problem during the trip was when she felt [　　14] because the boat was going so slowly.

Anna found the [　　15] in the Southern Ocean the most exciting part of the trip.

On her return, Anna phoned the [　　16] to ask for a certificate.

Anna's claim was doubted because she hadn't been in contact with people on [　　17] during her trip.

Anna's story was finally believed after her [　　18] had been checked.

▶ 填空练习

Interviewer: In the studio this week we have Anna Stephens, who returned last July after a _____ _____ round the world alone. Anna, welcome to the programme. Tell me how did you ____ _____ ___ _____?

Anna: Well, although I was a teacher of sports in a school _____ ____ _____, it _____ _____ I _____ _____ for a _____ _____ that I first ____ _____. A colleague invited me and I loved it _____. After that I went on several sailing holidays with friends in the Mediterranean.

Interviewer: So where did you get the idea to ____ _____ ___ _____ _____?

Anna: Well, I read a book, *High Adventure*, was the title, which was about a woman sailing alone, and it really _____ me. I suddenly knew what I wanted to do with my life. So I gave up my job and talked a friend into _____ __ ____ _____. It was a bit ____ _____ _____, but basically fine. I then _____ the next few months _____ the boat.

Interviewer: Did you take the boat out to sea to test it?

Anna: Well, that was the problem—I _____ _____ __ _____ three weeks _____ how the boat _____ at sea, but after six days I had to return because it ____ _____ in bad weather. That was good really because if I'd had three weeks of good weather I wouldn't have realised what problems I _____ __ _____ _____.

Interviewer: What did people say when you _____ ___ _____ _____?

Anna: Oh, some of them thought this proved I wasn't _____ ___ ____ _____. I _____ _____ _____ to ____ ___ ____ __ _____ without telling anybody, but because I _____ ___ _____ from a number of local companies, they all had ___ ___ ___ _____ __ ___ _____.

Interviewer: Right. Once you finally ____ _____ and you were out there alone, did you never ____ _____?

Anna: Well, yes I did, but that wasn't my main problem. The trip _____ _____ ___ _____ by the boat _____ ___ _____ _____ that I got bored. I wanted to be doing something all the time. The only time I really felt busy was in the Southern Ocean, where there were _____ _____ and I had plenty to think about all the time.

Interviewer: Were the storms _____ _____?

Anna: No, they were the really exciting part. My _____ _____ was when I got back home and people didn't believe I'd really done it.

Interviewer: Why did that happen?

Anna: Well, _____ _____ _____ __ _____, I got on the phone to the World Sailing Club to say that I had _____ _____ the trip and what did I have to do to ___ ____ _____. They told me to fill in all the forms, etc. Then, on television, people began to say that it was strange, although I _____ ___ _____ _____ around the world, I ___ ___ _____ ___ _____ ___ any ships along the way. That's what started it. After that the newspapers were saying I hadn't made the trip at all!

Interviewer: So how did you _____ ____ _____ people?

Anna: Well, I showed the sailing club my diaries, which I'd been very careful to keep _____ throughout the trip, and they checked them and gave me a certificate. I even ____ ____ _____ from the newspapers in the end.

Interviewer: And what will your next _____ ____?

Anna: I haven't got any _____ _____ as yet, but I'm writing a book about the trip.

Interviewer: Well, thank you, Anna. We look forward to reading all about it…

▶ 听力原文

Interviewer: In the studio this week we have Anna Stephens, who returned last July after a non-stop voyage round the world alone. Anna, welcome to the programme. Tell me how did you get interested in sailing?

Anna: Well, although I was a teacher of sports in a school for a while, it wasn't until I started working for a travel agency that I first went sailing. A colleague invited me and I loved it straightaway. After that I went on several sailing holidays with friends in the Mediterranean.

Interviewer: So where did you get the idea to sail round the world alone?

Anna: Well, I read a book, *High Adventure*, was the title, which was about a woman sailing alone, and it really impressed me. I suddenly knew what I wanted to do with my life. So I gave up my job and talked a friend into lending me his boat. It was a bit old and rusty, but basically fine. I then spent the next few months mending the boat.

Interviewer: Did you take the boat out to sea to test it?

Anna: Well, that was the problem—I had planned to spend three weeks seeing how the boat performed at sea, but after six days I had to return because it got damaged in bad weather. That was good really because if I'd had three weeks of good weather I wouldn't have realised what problems I needed to sort out.

Interviewer: What did people say when you had to turn back?

Anna: Oh, some of them thought this proved I wasn't ready for the trip. I would have preferred to carry on with my preparations without telling anybody, but because I relied on money from a number of local companies, they all had to be kept informed of my progress.

Interviewer: Right. Once you finally set out and you were out there alone, did you never feel lonely?

Anna: Well, yes I did, but that wasn't my main problem. The trip was ruined for me by the boat making such slow progress that I got bored. I wanted to be doing something all the time. The only time I really felt busy was in the Southern Ocean, where there were enormous storms and I had plenty to think about all the time.

Interviewer: Were the storms really frightening?

Anna: No, they were the really exciting part. My main difficulty was when I got back home and people didn't believe I'd really done it.

Interviewer: Why did that happen?

Anna: Well, as soon as I returned, I got on the phone to the World Sailing Club to say that I had successfully completed the trip and what did I have to do to get my certificate. They told me to fill in all the forms, etc. Then, on television, people began to say that it was strange, although I claimed to have sailed around the world, I had not been in touch with any ships along the way. That's what started it. After that the newspapers were saying I hadn't made the trip at all!

Interviewer: So how did you manage to convince people?

Anna: Well, I showed the sailing club my diaries, which I'd been very careful to keep up-to-date throughout the trip, and they checked them and gave me a certificate. I even got an apology from the newspapers in the end.

Interviewer: And what will your next challenge be?

Anna: I haven't got any firm plans as yet, but I'm writing a book about the trip.

Interviewer: Well, thank you, Anna. We look forward to reading all about it...

SECTION 3

▶ 听力原题

Part 2

You will hear an interview with a man who enjoys flying in a small aircraft called a microlight. For Questions 9–18, complete the sentences.

Before his retirement, Brian worked as a pilot for a company called [＿＿＿＿ 9] for a long time.

Brian feels like a bird when flying his microlight because he doesn't have a [＿＿＿＿ 10] around him.

Brian disagrees with the suggestion that steering a microlight is like steering a [＿＿＿＿ 11].

Brian's record-breaking flight ended in [＿＿＿＿ 12].

Brian organised his flight in advance to avoid needing other people as [＿＿＿＿ 13] on the way.

Brian's microlight was modified so that it could carry more [＿＿＿＿ 14] on board.

It took Brian [＿＿＿＿ 15] to plan the record-breaking flight.

Brian feels that flying over miles and miles of [＿＿＿＿ 16] was the most dangerous part of the trip.

Brian describes his navigation system as both [＿＿＿＿ 17] and easy to use.

Brian says that his main problem on the flight was the fact that he became very [＿＿＿＿ 18].

▶ 填空练习

Interviewer: Now, today I have with me Brian Coleford, and he's someone who spends a lot of time up in the air in that smallest of aircraft, the microlight. Hello, Brian.

Brian: Hello.

Interviewer: But It's _____ ____ ____ __ _____, isn't it?

Brian: Oh yes. I learnt to fly when I was at university and I worked as a British Airways pilot for many years until my _____. These days I _____ a lot of my time _____ _____ who want to learn how to _____ ___ _____, as well as other _____ ___ _____, at a local flying club.

Interviewer: Tell us about the microlight.

Brian: Well, it's like a very small aircraft, which __ _____ ___ __ _____. The thing with microlight flying is that it's the closest you can get to _____ _____ like a bird, because you're _____ in the _____ _____—there's no cabin or anything around you.

Interviewer: Oh I see…

Brian: And _____ ___ _____, the way it's _____ is by moving your own weight. You _____ __ by _____ _____ _____ ____ _____ ___ _____.

Interviewer: So you have to lean over like you would on a motorbike?

Brian: You don't lean really, you actually _____ ___ _____. So you have to be quite fit, _____ ___ __ _____ _____.

Interviewer: Which brings us on to the other thing which I know about you, and that is that you've _____ _____ __ _____ _____. Tell us about that.

Brian: Well, it _____ _____ ____ _____ _____, because I left from London and _____ _____ Europe, Africa and Asia on the way to Australia. No one _____ _____ _____ that before in a microlight.

Interviewer: The _____ for a long flight must ___ _____ _____ _____, Brian. Surely you didn't do it all on your own?

Brian: Yes. I had ___ _____. It was __ _____ __ _____ __ _____ ____ _____ and finding out where I'd be able to _____ _____ enroute, and knowing how far I could plan to _____ _____ each day.

Interviewer: So how far can you travel on ___ _____ __ _____?

Brian: Well, I had a special _____ _____ _____—that was the only way in which my microlight was _____ for the flight. So that meant I had enough fuel to be able to do about eight hours. The _____ _____ I _____ _____ on the winds of course, but the _____ _____ was round about five hundred miles a day. It _____ nine months ___ _____ the forty-nine-day flight, and for each leg I ____ __ _____ ____, so that each airport I would land at knew that I was on the way, and if I _____ _____ _____ half an hour of the time I'd stated, then they'd have started looking for me.

Interviewer: Yes, I'm sure that's very _____. What radio, if any, did you have?

Brian: Yes, I had a two-way VHF radio, but the range of that was only seventy miles, so there was a lot of time when I was out of radio _____ _____ anybody. I _____ _____ __ _____ of _____ and _____, which is quite dangerous, of course, should anything go wrong, and five thousand miles of the trip was over the sea, which is even more so.

Interviewer: So how did you find your way?

Brian: Well, I had a _____ _____ which ____ _____ _____. It was really easy to use and, I must say, very _____. I couldn't say I had any problems in _____ _____ ___ _____ or _____ _____ I was going.

Interviewer: And what _____ ___ _____ did you have? I mean, you weren't just _____ ___ the cold air, were you?

Brian: Yeah, I just wear a _____ _____ _____ and warm clothes _____. The coldest was going over the Alps—it was _____ twenty-eight _____ there because I was quite _____ ____. But actually _____ ____ was my real problem because it ___ ____ _____ by the time I landed and I was leaving again at _____ _____. I was never hungry because I was met by _____ _____ _____ everywhere I went. Although sadly I didn't get to see much of the places I visited.

Interviewer: Well, Brian, many congratulations. It's a wonderful achievement. And thank you very much for coming in today and talking about…

▶ 听力原文

Interviewer: Now, today I have with me Brian Coleford, and he's someone who spends a lot of time up in the air in that smallest of aircraft, the microlight. Hello, Brian.

Brian: Hello.

Interviewer: But It's more than just a hobby, isn't it?

Brian: Oh yes. I learnt to fly when I was at university and I worked as a British Airways pilot for many years until my retirement. These days I spend a lot of my time helping people who want to learn how to fly a microlight, as well as other types of aircraft, at a local flying club.

Interviewer: Tell us about the microlight.

Brian: Well, it's like a very small aircraft, which is powered by an engine. The thing with microlight flying is that it's the closest you can get to actually feeling like a bird, because you're out in the open air—there's no cabin or anything around you.

Interviewer: Oh I see…

Brian: And although it's powered, the way it's controlled is by moving your own weight. You steer it by moving your body one way or another.

Interviewer: So you have to lean over like you would on a motorbike?

Brian: You don't lean really, you actually have to push. So you have to be quite fit, especially for a long flight.

Interviewer: Which brings us on to the other thing which I know about you, and that is that you've recently broken a world record. Tell us about that.

Brian: Well, it involved flying over four continents, because I left from London and flew over Europe, Africa and Asia on the way to Australia. No one had ever done that before in a microlight.

Interviewer: The organisation for a long flight must be very difficult indeed, Brian. Surely you didn't do it all on your own?

Brian: Yes. I had no helpers. It was a matter of planning my route in advance and finding out where I'd be able to get fuel enroute, and knowing how far I could plan to travel safely each day.

Interviewer: So how far can you travel on one tank of fuel?

Brian: Well, I had a special fuel tank fitted—that was the only way in which my microlight was modified for the flight. So that meant I had enough fuel to be able to do about eight hours. The actual distance I covered depended on the winds of course, but the still-air distance was round about five hundred miles a day. It took nine months to plan the forty-nine-day flight, and for each leg I filed a flight plan, so that each airport I would land at knew that I was on the way, and if I didn't arrive within half an hour of the time I'd stated, then they'd have started looking for me.

Interviewer: Yes, I'm sure that's very necessary. What radio, if any, did you have?

Brian: Yes, I had a two-way VHF radio, but the range of that was only seventy miles, so there was a lot of time when I was out of radio contact with anybody. I crossed thousands of miles of desert and mountain, which is quite dangerous, of course, should anything go wrong, and five thousand miles of the trip was over the sea, which is even more so.

Interviewer: So how did you find your way?

Brian: Well, I had a navigation system which uses satellite signals. It was really easy to use and, I must say, very accurate. I couldn't say I had any problems in knowing where I was or which way I was going.

Interviewer: And what sort of protection did you have? I mean, you weren't just dangling in the cold air, were you?

Brian: Yeah, I just wear a warm flying suit and warm clothes underneath. The coldest was going over the Alps—it was minus twenty-eight degrees there because I was quite high up. But actually feeling tired was my real problem because it was often dark by the time I landed and I was leaving again at first light. I was never hungry because I was met by such great hospitality everywhere I went. Although sadly I didn't get to see much of the places I visited.

Interviewer: Well, Brian, many congratulations. It's a wonderful achievement. And thank you very much for coming in today and talking about…

SECTION 4

▶ 听力原题

Part 2

You will hear part of a radio programme in which a woman called Sylvia Short is interviewed about her job. For Questions 9–18, complete the sentences.

Sylvia studied [and | **9**] at university.

After university, Sylvia worked as a [| **10**] in Italy.

The company which employs Sylvia is called [| **11**].

Sylvia worked for the company for [| **12**] before becoming the manager's assistant.

Part of Sylvia's job is to organise the [| **13**] in newspapers and magazines.

Sylvia often has to deal with strange questions from [| **14**].

Sylvia's boss has a radio show on Fridays on the subject of [| **15**].

Sylvia has written about her [| **16**] for a new book on Britain.

Sylvia says that in the future she would like to be a [| **17**] on television.

Last year, Sylvia enjoyed attending a [| **18**] in Australia.

▶ 填空练习

Interviewer: Good morning, and today we are _____ ____ our _____ __ _____ for young people. In the studio today we have Sylvia Short, who works for a company that _____ _____ for serious travellers. Now, Sylvia, I believe you left Essex University with __ _____ ___ _____ and _____. Tell us something about how you got your job.

Sylvia: My main interest has always been travel. I _____ every holiday when I was a student _____ _____. After I left university I spent a year as an English teacher in Spain, _____ by six months as a _____ _____ in Italy. When I _____ to England I _____ ____ _____ ___ jobs _____ in the newspaper, but didn't have _____ _____. So I _____ to make __ ___ ___ every company I wanted to work for and write to them directly, rather than ____ ____ them to advertise.

Interviewer: Good _____ to anyone, I think.

Sylvia: Yes, and I was very _____ as the company World Travel needed an _____ in their office in London. I ____ ____ ____ __ _____ ___ _____, just to ____ _____ __ ____ ____ __ _____ _____. _____, I was _____ to do more, but I wasn't __ __ _____. Then the manager's assistant _____ she was leaving after only _____ ____ the company for twelve months, and I _____ ____ her job. The company _____ their _____ __ _____ ___ higher-level jobs, and I was _____ four months after joining.

Interviewer: Good for you! What does the job _____?

Sylvia: Well, I've _____ __ _____ since I took it on. I'm __ _____ __ all the advertising in the _____ whenever we _____ __ ____ _____ and I sometimes give talks to people in the _____ _____.

Interview: Do you find the work _____?

Sylvia: Oh, yes, it's never boring. We often get ____ _____ ____ _____. They _____ we know everything there is to know about travel so they often _____ ____ __ ____ if we can help them. One rang to say he was writing an article and wanted to know whether there were any _____ _____ _____ in China.

Interviewer: Really? And what other things do you find yourself doing?

Sylvia: Oh, a large part of my job is to _____ _____ my boss is where she should be. She does a lot of TV interviews on all _____ of travel and she also _____ a radio programme ____ _____ _____ every Friday night. In between she writes articles and now and again _____ ___ ____ _____ to find out what's going on there. My job is to _____ ___ _____ _____.

Interviewer: What do you think you've _____ _____ working for her?

Sylvia: Oh, she's an _____ writer and she's helped me, _____ when I have to do _____ _____—she suggests changes, but she's very _____, not _____. She even suggested I did part of a chapter in a new guidebook to Great Britain on my hometown, which I enjoyed a lot.

interviewer: So, how do you see your _____ _____?

Sylvia: Well, I don't think I'm _____ _____ to be __ _____ _____. But my boss has a lot of _____ in the TV world, and I ____ _____ _ ___ _____. However, at the moment I'm enjoying my job ___ ___ ___ __ ___ __ ___.

Interviewer: Do you get to go abroad as _____ ____ _____ _____?

Sylvia: Not as often as you'd think! I ___ _____ a lot of time _____ things like answering the phone, but I ____ _____ to go to the company's _____ _____ in Australia last year for __ _____. That was _____.

Interviewer: Sounds to me like you've got the perfect job, Sylvia! Next…

● 听力原文

Interviewer: Good morning, and today we are continuing with our series on careers for young people. In the studio today we have Sylvia Short, who works for a company that produces guidebooks for serious travellers. Now, Sylvia, I believe you left Essex University with a degree in German and Spanish. Tell us something about how you got your job.

Sylvia: My main interest has always been travel. I spent every holiday when I was a student travelling abroad. After I left university I spent a year as an English teacher in Spain, followed by six months as a tour guide in Italy. When I returned to England I applied for loads of jobs advertised in the newspaper, but didn't have any success. So I decided to make a list of every company I wanted to work for and write to them directly, rather than wait for them to advertise.

Interviewer: Good advice to anyone, I think.

Sylvia: Yes, and I was very lucky as the company World Travel needed an assistant in their office in London. I dealt mainly with the post at first, just to get used to their way of doing things. Obviously, I was qualified to do more, but I wasn't in a hurry. Then the manager's assistant announced she was leaving after only being with the company for twelve months, and I applied for her job. The company encourages their staff to apply for higher-level jobs, and I was promoted four months after joining.

Interviewer: Good for you! What does the job involve?

Sylvia: Well, I've expanded the role since I took it on. I'm in charge of all the advertising in the press whenever we publish a new guidebook and I sometimes give talks to people in the travel industry.

Interview: Do you find the work interesting?

Sylvia: Oh, yes, it's never boring. We often get odd requests from journalists. They assume we know everything there is to know about travel so they often ring us to see if we can help them. One rang to say he was writing an article and wanted to know whether there were any female football teams in China.

Interviewer: Really? And what other things do you find yourself doing?

Sylvia: Oh, a large part of my job is to make sure my boss is where she should be. She does a lot of TV interviews on all aspects of travel and she also presents a radio programme about adventure holidays every Friday night. In between she writes articles and now and again comes into the office to find out what's going on there. My job is to keep her fully informed.

Interviewer: What do you think you've learnt from working for her?

Sylvia: Oh, she's an excellent writer and she's helped me, especially when I have to do press releases—she suggests changes, but she's very encouraging, not bossy. She even suggested I did part of a chapter in a new guidebook to Great Britain on my hometown, which I enjoyed a lot.

interviewer: So, how do you see your career developing?

Sylvia: Well, I don't think I'm good enough to be a full-time writer. But my boss has a lot of contacts in the TV world, and I fancy becoming a TV presenter. However, at the moment I'm enjoying my job far too much to give it up.

Interviewer: Do you get to go abroad as part of your job?

Sylvia: Not as often as you'd think! I do spend a lot of time doing things like answering the phone, but I did manage to go to the company's head office in Australia last year for a conference. That was terrific.

Interviewer: Sounds to me like you've got the perfect job, Sylvia! Next…

CHAPTER 3 FCE LISTENING PART 3

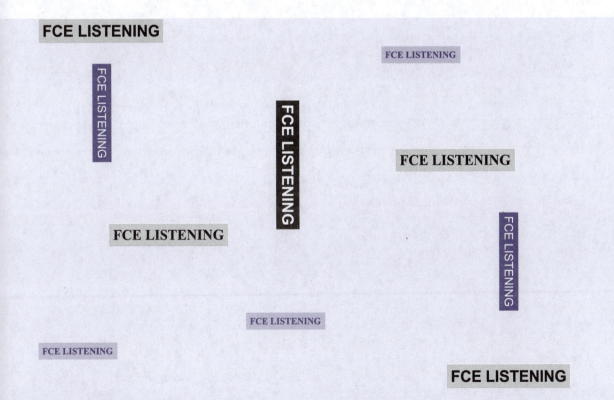

SECTION 1

▶ 听力原题

Part 3

You will hear five different people talking about their work on a cruise ship. For Questions 19–23, choose from the list (A–F) what each speaker says about their work. Use the letters only once. There is one extra letter which you do not need to use.

A. One aspect of my job is less interesting than others.

| Speaker 1 | 19 |

B. My job involves planning for the unexpected.

| Speaker 2 | 20 |

C. You have to be sociable to do my job.

| Speaker 3 | 21 |

D. I don't like routine in my working life.

| Speaker 4 | 22 |

E. There's not much work to do during the day.

| Speaker 5 | 23 |

F. I provide passengers with a souvenir of their trip.

▶ 填空练习

Speaker 1

I _____ _____ anything to do with _____ on board, and that _____ _____ _____, _____ _____, the show company and any _____ _____. I have to plan each _____ with all the _____ and then _____ them at the _____ of the ____. There's never __ _____ _____! And if I want time to myself I have to _____ __ ___ ____, because a huge part of my job is to ___ ____ _____. There are often parties to attend…and then, sometimes, _____ _____ __ _____. So, if I'm not in the shows, I'll be out there _____ ___ ___ _____, because that's ____ __ ___ ___ too.

Speaker 2

I'm ___ _____ ___ _____ at the Health and Fitness Centre, so I _____ _____ and
_____ ____ _____ _____ programmes and _____ _____. I wouldn't say it was
_____ because it's very hard work, but the _____ for me are _____ _____ _____ _____,
and the _____ ___ working. We do _____ _____, and once you've finished, it's _____ ____
_____ how much time you _____ ____. Then you _____ ____ _____ when you're ready.
I like _____ __ __ _____ _____. I don't like to feel ___ ____ ____ ____ _____.
At home, everyone _____ ___ ____ _____ _____. Here, time just _____ ___
_____ _____.

Speaker 3

I'm _____ ___ ____ _____ of the passengers. That means that, _____ _____ _____
__ ____ __ ____ on a day-to-day basis, I have to _____ _____ that passengers _____ ____
_____ _____ if there's an _____. So I do a lot of _____ _____ to _____ _____
____ _____ __ _____ _____ _____ what to do if there's a problem…and, of course, we do
_____ _____ ____ __ _____. In theory, I'm on call for twenty-four hours a day, but, in
fact, I'm _____ ___ ____ for about fifteen, so I do ___ ____ _____ __ _____ a bit
too. When we're in port, though, I get _____ _____ ____ _____.

Speaker 4

There are six photographers here, and we take photos of passengers in _____ _____ on the ship. My
main _____, though, is to _____ and _____ all the passenger film, so I'm _____ ____ _____
_____. We don't have set hours because every _____ programme is different and, because I _____
____ _____, I _____ _____ ____ _____ until six in the morning—_____ ____ _____
for the next day. It's quite _____. People like having their pictures _____ ____ ____ _____,
and we also do quite a ____ _____ ____ ___ _____ and ___ _____ _____, but generally people
come to us with their _____ _____.

Speaker 5

I'm ____ _____ ___ all the restaurants ____ _____. So, _____, _____ and the _____
of food, plus any _____ _____—it's all _____ ___ ____. I love all that, _____ ___ ___ _____ and
_____ can be ___ _____ _____ _____. But I've _____ for this company for _____
twenty-four years, and I _____ _____ it for one minute. Even though we can't _____
_____ ___ _____, we can put in _____ ____ _____ _____. So, _____, I do four
months away and then two months leave. Where else could you get a job like that and _____ _____
_____ it? You miss your friends and family, but you don't get time to think about it.

▶ 听力原文

Speaker 1

I deal with anything to do with entertainment on board, and that covers guest lectures, cabaret artists, the show company and any special nights. I have to plan each cruise with all the performers and then introduce them at the beginning of the show. There's never a dull moment! And if I want time to myself I have to escape to my cabin, because a huge part of my job is to mix with people. There are often parties to attend…and then, sometimes, dance nights to organise. So, if I'm not in the shows, I'll be out there dancing with the passengers, because that's part of my job too.

Speaker 2

I'm in charge of reception at the Health and Fitness Centre, so I greet passengers and organise their individual fitness programmes and beauty treatments. I wouldn't say it was glamorous because it's very hard work, but the rewards for me are meeting really interesting people, and the system of working. We do eight-month contracts, and once you've finished, it's up to you how much time you have off. Then you renew your contract when you're ready. I like working on a contract basis. I don't like to feel as if I'm stuck somewhere. At home, everyone follows the same nine-to-five pattern. Here, time just has a different meaning.

Speaker 3

I'm responsible for the safety of the passengers. That means that, apart from keeping an eye on things on a day-to-day basis, I have to make sure that passengers can be safely evacuated if there's an emergency. So I do a lot of staff training to make sure each member of staff knows exactly what to do if there's a problem…and, of course, we do emergency drills with the passengers. In theory, I'm on call for twenty-four hours a day, but, in fact, I'm generally on duty for about fifteen, so I do get the chance to socialise a bit too. When we're in port, though, I get the whole time off.

Speaker 4

There are six photographers here, and we take photos of passengers in various locations on the ship. My main role, though, is to develop and print all the passenger film, so I'm less in evidence socially. We don't have set hours because every cruise programme is different and, because I print the photos, I frequently carry on working until six in the morning—getting them ready for the next day. It's quite exciting. People like having their pictures taken with the captain, and we also do quite a few shots in the restaurant and on party nights, but generally people come to us with their own requests.

Speaker 5

I'm in charge of all the restaurants on board. So, menus, costings and the quality of food, plus any staff issues—it's all down to me. I love all that, even if the paperwork and counts can be a bit dull sometimes. But I've worked for this company for nearly twenty-four years, and I haven't regretted it for one minute. Even though we can't choose where we go, we can put in requests for certain cruises. So, normally, I do four months away and then two months leave. Where else could you get a job like that and get paid for it? You miss your friends and family, but you don't get time to think about it.

SECTION 2

▶ 听力原题

Part 3

You will hear five young people talking about what makes a good teacher. For Questions 19–23, choose from the list (A–F) which of the opinions each speaker expresses. Use the letters only once. There is one extra letter which you do not need to use.

A. A good teacher praises effort.

Speaker 1 |____| 19

B. A good teacher knows the subject well.

Speaker 2 |____| 20

C. A good teacher is strict.

Speaker 3 |____| 21

D. A good teacher is available outside the classroom.

Speaker 4 |____| 22

E. A good teacher is entertaining.

Speaker 5 |____| 23

F. A good teacher has experience.

▶ 填空练习

Speaker 1

Well, we've had lots of teachers who really _____ _____ _____. I mean, you could ask any question and you knew you'd get the answer. But most teachers, when their class _____ _____, that was it, they were gone. You see, a teacher may know a lot. _____ _____ ____, it's usually after class that ____ _____ _____ _____, often as ____ _____, if you know what I mean. They think if they just _____ _____ and do the job, that's _____ _____. I remember one teacher, she was new, said _____ ____ _____ _____. I liked that. I really did…

Speaker 2

I was always _____ ____ _____, and I think it was because I had this _____ teacher, I was lucky really. I didn't like doing my homework, and he'd say 'These are the rules, take it or leave it, you do this for tomorrow or you're out of my class'. You see, a teacher may be there for you _____ ____ _____ ____ _____, but if he doesn't _____ ____ __ ____ _____ _____, it'll all be _____, _____ ___? This teacher _____ _____ in the school for many, many years, and I know some of the younger teachers _____ _____ ___ _____.

Speaker 3

I think it _____ ____ _____ for a teacher ___ _____ really good. Sometimes a teacher who's just _____, well, they_____ ___ ___ _____, _____ a lot, it's as if they want to teach you everything now, if you know what I mean. Some of my friends were always _____ ___ _____ who'd been there ____ __ _____ and I used to say, 'Well, they're the ones who've gone through all this before and when they tell me I've done something really well, it _____ a lot, _____ ____?'

Speaker 4

In my opinion, a good teacher has to _____ _____ _____ _____ __ _____ _____. I once had a history teacher who was _____ _____ ____ _____—you know, her _____, her _____, like a big sister, she was. I ____ very _____ ___ history at the time, and I realised she didn't exactly…_____ ____ _____…I think this kind of ____ __ _____, although she was always _____ __ _____ _____ __ for me in her library, nothing was ____ ____ _____ for her. But I _____ ___ ____ _____ in her.

Speaker 5

No matter how much a teacher _____ _____ __ _____, I think he or she_____ ___ _____ that the students are not there to _____ _____. A good teacher is one that _____ _____ all the time, who tells you when you're _____ _____, even if it's only very _____ _____. Of course, a person can know _____ _____ __ _____ and still be no good as a teacher. We've all had teachers like that, the kind who'll only __ _____ ____ __ _____ _____ and who will never _____ ____ _____ for having tried.

▶ 听力原文

Speaker 1

Well, we've had lots of teachers who really knew their stuff. I mean, you could ask any question and you knew you'd get the answer. But most teachers, when their class was over, that was it, they were gone. You see, a teacher may know a lot. The thing is, it's usually after class that you need their help, often as an individual, if you know what I mean. They think if they just turn up and do the job, that's good enough. I remember one teacher, she was new, said drop in any time. I liked that. I really did…

Speaker 2

I was always good at math, and I think it was because I had this excellent teacher, I was lucky really. I didn't like doing my homework, and he'd say 'These are the rules, take it or leave it, you do this for tomorrow or you're out of my class'. You see, a teacher may be there for you whenever you need his advice, but if he doesn't force you to do your best, it'll all be wasted, won't it? This teacher had been in the school for many, many years, and I know some of the younger teachers didn't like his methods.

Speaker 3

I think it takes some time for a teacher to become really good. Sometimes a teacher who's just starting, well, they can be so demanding, expect a lot, it's as if they want to teach you everything now, if you know what I mean. Some of my friends were always against the teachers who'd been there for a while and I used to say, 'Well, they're the ones who've gone through all this before and when they tell me I've done something really well, it means a lot, doesn't it?'

Speaker 4

In my opinion, a good teacher has to be able to cover a topic thoroughly. I once had a history teacher who was really kind and helpful—you know, her smile, her manner, like a big sister, she was. I was very interested in history at the time, and I realised she didn't exactly…master the subject…I think this kind of put me off, although she was always willing to look things up for me in her library, nothing was too much trouble for her. But I sort of lost confidence in her.

Speaker 5

No matter how much a teacher knows about a subject, I think he or she needs to remember that the students are not there to become experts. A good teacher is one that gives encouragement all the time, who tells you when you're making progress, even if it's only very little progress. Of course, a person can know everything about a subject and still be no good as a teacher. We've all had teachers like that, the kind who'll only be satisfied with the highest standards and who will never give you credit for having tried.

SECTION 3

▶ 听力原题

Part 3

You will hear five different people talking about short courses they have attended. For Questions 19–23, choose from the list(A–F) what each speaker says about their course. Use the letters only once. There is one extra letter which you do not need to use.

A. I was encouraged by the teachers to continue developing my skill.

Speaker 1 | 19

B. I learnt something about the subject that I hadn't expected.

Speaker 2 | 20

C. I preferred the social life to the course content.

Speaker 3 | 21

D. I intend doing a similar course again.

Speaker 4 | 22

E. I found out something about myself.

Speaker 5 | 23

F. I thought the course was good value for money.

▶ 填空练习

Speaker 1

I went on a _____ _____ last weekend, _____ _____ ___ _____ _____, because _____ ___ ____ _____, I thought canoeing _____ __ ____ _____. And I was right. I really _____ ____ ___ _____ ___ __. I ___ the _____ ____ _____ ___: not because I was one of their star students, far from it, but I ____ ___ __ ___ _____ ____ often than everyone else put together! But even so, I _____ ___ ___ _____ _____ _____ _____ __ ____ group _____ ___ to do another course together, in six months' time, I found myself _____ __ too. I bet the tutors _____ __ ____ ___ _____ _____!

Speaker 2

It was really ____ ____: fifteen people from all ____ __ _____, all _____ _____ __ _____ _____ to each other, and most of us were _____ _____. We ____ _____ ____ _____, but _____ it did ___ __ ____ _____ ___ ____ ____ ____, and the tutors were _____ _____. It ____ ____ in a big house in the country which now _____ ___ __ _____, and the whole thing ___ _____. In fact, I don't know how they can do it for _____ ____ _____, because it was almost like staying in a _____ ____. Maybe it __ _____ ___ ___ _____.

Speaker 3

It was quite an ____ _____ ___ _____, in a way, because I _____ _____ ___ __ _____ together, and _____ ___ _____ ___ ____, but most of the time we were all just working on our own computers, with the tutor _____ _____ and _____ ___ _____ _____. No teamwork at all. It made me realise that I work much _____ ___ ____ ____ ____ on my own: maybe it's ____ _____, or something. Anyway, I _____ ____ ____ ____ _____ __ _____, which is what I wanted, so I _____ ___ ____ _____ it, even though I can't say I ____ ___ _____.

Speaker 4

I can _____ ____. I'm so _____. We were out ___ _____ _____ _____ tennis from morning to night, _____. I'm _____ not ___ ____ ___ I ____ __ __. I suppose they thought we'd want to play all day to ____ ___ _____ ____. Well, I ____ _____ ____ with a bit more _____ ___ _____ and a lot more taking it easy! They told me I should go on to ___ _____ _____, next month, but I don't know: I think they have to say that to get ___ _____, because they _____ ___ __ _____ the same thing to everyone.

Speaker 5

There were several people I've met on other courses: I _____ _____ ___ ____ _____, but some of them _____ __ ____ __ _____ __ _____ __ ____. Actually we ____ ___ _____ a lot of time _____ and ____ for walks in the garden, and that kind of ___ __ ___ ___ ____ ____ I didn't really learn much about ___ ____, which is why I'd gone. The ____ _____ ____ __ ___ ____ __ _____, but she ____ __ ____ ___ little idea how to teach so I just couldn't get into it. And it cost enough. I _____ ___ ___ _____ a better way of studying.

◉ 听力原文

Speaker 1

I went on a canoeing course last weekend, rather against my better judgement, because although I enjoy swimming, I thought canoeing might be too difficult. And I was right. I really couldn't get the hang of it. I bet the tutors will remember me: not because I was one of their star students, far from it, but I fell out of the canoe more often than everyone else put together! But even so, I enjoyed it so much that when some of the group signed up to do another course together, in six months' time, I found myself signing up too. I bet the tutors refuse to teach me next time!

Speaker 2

It was really good fun: fifteen people from all sorts of backgrounds, all desperately trying to speak Italian to each other, and most of us were absolute beginners. We kept falling about laughing, but actually it did get a lot easier by the last day, and the tutors were awfully patient. It was held in a big house in the country which now belongs to a university, and the whole thing was brilliant. In fact, I don't know how they can do it for what they charged, because it was almost like staying in a luxury hotel. Maybe it was subsidised by the university.

Speaker 3

It was quite an odd sort of course, in a way, because I expected everyone to be working together, and helping each other to learn, but most of the time we were all just working on our own computers, with the tutor going round and helping each person individually. No teamwork at all. It made me realise that I work much better with other people than on my own: maybe it's poor motivation, or something. Anyway, I learnt much more about using a computer, which is what I wanted, so I suppose it was worth it, even though I can't say I enjoyed it much.

Speaker 4

I can hardly move. I'm so exhausted. We were out on the courts playing tennis from morning to night, practically. I'm certainly not as fit as I ought to be. I suppose they thought we'd want to play all day to get our money's worth. Well, I could have done with a bit more theory and demonstrations and a lot more taking it easy! They told me I should go on to the advanced course, next month, but I don't know: I think they have to say that to get the bookings, because they seemed to be saying the same thing to everyone.

Speaker 5

There were several people I've met on other courses: I haven't been on that many, but some of them seemed to take at least a dozen a year. Actually we ended up spending a lot of time chatting and going for walks in the garden, and that kind of made up for the fact that I didn't really learn much about local history, which is why I'd gone. The tutor certainly knew a lot about the subject, but she seemed to have very little idea how to teach so I just couldn't get into it. And it cost enough. I probably need to find a better way of studying.

SECTION 4

▶ 听力原题

Part 3

You will hear five different people speaking on the subject of motorbikes. For Questions 19–23, choose the phrase(A–F) which best summerises what each speaker is talking about. Use the letters only once. There is one extra letter which you do not need to use.

A. the perfect passenger

Speaker 1 | 19

B. a feeling of power

Speaker 2 | 20

C. a lengthy career

Speaker 3 | 21

D. the best way to learn

Speaker 4 | 22

E. a family business

Speaker 5 | 23

F. a break with routine

▶ 填空练习

Speaker 1

There's _____ ____ _____ __ __ _____, it's wonderful. All my life, I've never _____ ___ _____ ____. I was _____ _____ __ _____ when I first _____ ___ __ _____ ____. I had my _____ in nineteen fifty-five and when a company in Birmingham _____ ___ __ ___ _____ ___ _____ and got it. I had to ride all the bikes they made from nineteen fifty-seven through to nineteen seventy-eight, which _____ _____ _____, _____ _____ and _____ _____. After the company closed down, I did _____ _____ with my brother. We called ourselves The Partners Dare, but by then, of course, it was only a hobby.

Speaker 2

Well, of course, although many people ____ ____ ____ _____, fathers or other _____ _____ who ride, actually before you go on the road at all in Britain, you've got to _____ __ _____ _____ course, and that really gets you off on the right foot. Now, after you've _____ that, you're _____ on the road, but we as an _____ _____ _____ that you ____ _____ _____, and this may be where Dad can help, you know. Then, after that, of course, you're _____ _____ to buy what you like, go on _____, take _____, and just _____ _____ _____.

Speaker 3

I've __ _____ ___ my bike because it takes me away from the day-to-day _____ __ _____ _____, as a mother, and the problems of that _____ ____ _____. I can just put the key in, turn it, and I'm in another world. And I _____ ____ _____ ___ ___ ____ _____ and _____ just by riding my bike. Then, you may be going _____ ___ _____ and, if cars are _____ you, you do see the women sort of turn, and you can ____ ____ them saying 'you look great' or 'well done' and the men always give you ___ _____ ___ ____ _____.

Speaker 4

The motorbike seems to be an _____ _____ _____. This is because it is the _____ _____ ___ _____ for the _____. You don't have to ____ _____ ___ ____ _____ person, you can ____ _____ _____, on a very _____ _____, but there's also the idea of the ____ ___ _____, _____ and _____. It's really the ____ of _____ _____, the sense of _____ _____ ___ _____ of your own _____—it's just great fun. You must do it; it's wonderful. You'll enjoy _____ _____ of it.

Speaker 5

My mother bought me a bike as soon as I had my _____ and she ____ __ _____ _____ ___ _____ on the back in those days. And then when I _____ _____ _____, she used to come with me as the side-car partner. In those days we did a lot of races together—just for fun. She was wonderful, the same _____ as me, so the _____ was _____, and she used to enjoy it. I don't know _____ ____ ____ __ ____ family really thought about it, but my brothers are _____ _____ now. Their wives won't let them ride motorbikes, so they look _____ at mine sometimes.

▶ 听力原文

Speaker 1

There's nothing like getting on a motorbike, it's wonderful. All my life, I've never travelled any other way. I was eleven years of age when I first started on my brother's bike. I had my license in nineteen fifty-five and when a company in Birmingham advertised for a test rider I applied and got it. I had to ride all the bikes they made from nineteen fifty-seven through to nineteen seventy-eight, which included hill climbs, reliability trials and speedway races. After the company closed down, I did trick riding with my brother. We called ourselves The Partners Dare, but by then, of course, it was only a hobby.

Speaker 2

Well, of course, although many people start off with brothers, fathers or other family members who ride, actually before you go on the road at all in Britain, you've got to take a basic training course, and that really gets you off on the right foot. Now, after you've passed that, you're allowed on the road, but we as an organisation strongly recommend that you take further training, and this may be where Dad can help, you know. Then, after that, of course, you're completely free to buy what you like, go on motorways, take passengers, and just thoroughly enjoy motorcycling.

Speaker 3

I've a passion for my bike because it takes me away from the day-to-day round of family life, as a mother, and the problems of that kind of existence. I can just put the key in, turn it, and I'm in another world. And I can be relieved of all the stresses and strains just by riding my bike. Then, you may be going along the motorway and, if cars are passing you, you do see the women sort of turn, and you can lip read them saying 'you look great' or 'well done' and the men always give you a wave in the mirror.

Speaker 4

The motorbike seems to be an incredibly strong image. This is because it is the perfect form of transport for the individual. You don't have to take account of any other person, you can cut through traffic, on a very simple level, but there's also the idea of the unity of mind, body and machine. It's really the sense of complete freedom, the sense of being completely in control of your own destiny—it's just great fun. You must do it; it's wonderful. You'll enjoy every minute of it.

Speaker 5

My mother bought me a bike as soon as I had my license and she used to ride thousands of miles on the back in those days. And then when I started side-car competitions, she used to come with me as the side-car partner. In those days we did a lot of races together—just for fun. She was wonderful, the same weight as me, so the balance was marvelous, and she used to enjoy it. I don' t know what the rest of the family really thought about it, but my brothers are deeply admiring now. Their wives won't let them ride motorbikes, so they look lovingly at mine sometimes.

CHAPTER 4 FCE LISTENING PART 4

FCE LISTENING

FCE LISTENING

FCE LISTENING

FCE LISTENING

FCE LISTENING

FCE LISTENING

FCE LISTENING

FCE LISTENING

FCE LISTENING

FCE LISTENING

SECTION 1

▶ 听力原题

Part 4

You will hear an interview with a man called Stan Leach who is talking about adventure sports. For Questions 24–30, choose the best answer (A, B or C).

24   Stan says that the best thing about walking is that you can

A. be safe by doing it.

B. please yourself how you do it.

C. do it on your own.

25   Stan's opinion on scrambling is that

A. people doing it may need to be accompanied.

B. it is unsuitable for beginners.

C. it is more interesting than walking.

26   What did Stan discover when he went climbing?

A. It was far from fun.

B. It was harder than he expected.

C. It can be very frightening.

27   What does Stan say about mountain biking?

A. America has special cycling paths.

B. It is more expensive in Britain than elsewhere.

C. It is best where there are lots of downhill slopes.

28   Stan's advice on scuba diving is that

A. most people can not breathe normally.

B. it is easier than it seems.

C. you should think carefully before trying it.

29   What is Stan's view of skydiving?

A. It is surprisingly popular.

B. It is best to join a team.

C. Only certain types of people like it.

30　What does Stan say about canoeing?

A. You can do it in conditions that suit you.

B. It is best for a beginner to practice in a stretch.

C. There are few places in Britain to do it.

▶ 填空练习

Interviewer: …Welcome back to the programme. Well, _____ _____ that the _____ sports in Britain are _____ _____, and I have with me Stan Leach, an _____ at the _____ _____, who's going to tell us a bit about some of them. Stan, where shall we start?

Stan: Well, most people _____ _____ _____, I think—although of course _____ _____ it's not _____ ___ _____ ____, but it's what ____ _____ _____ _____. Indeed, the great thing about walking in Britain is the _____ _____, from an _____ _____ to a _____ ____, to an _____ _____ ____ __ ____ _____. If you want to _____ ____ _____, you can start with a few_____ _____ _____ and then _____ something _____ and _____ _____.

Interviewer: What's this thing called _____ I've been _____ about?

Stan: Yeah, scrambling is _____ __ ____ ____ _____ ____ between walking and climbing. Scrambles are _____ _____ ___ _____, and on the harder ones, which are _____ ____ to _____ _____. It's best to go with an _____.

Interviewer: Well, that brings us _____ ____ ___ _____—that's really _____ ___ _____ _____, hasn't it?

Stan: Yes, and of course you know it _____ _____ ___ _____ _____ ___ ____ _____ ____ ones like _____. Climbing _____ _____ ___ _____ to begin with, but it's great fun and really_____ ____ ___. You start by climbing small _____ before moving on to a _____ _____. I went for a day's lesson with _____ Alan Kimber in Scotland and it was really _____ but_____ _____.

Interviewer: Right, well, what's next?

Stan: Mountain biking. If you can _____ _____ ___ _____ _____, you can _____ _____ Britain. But unlike in the USA, where there are _____ _____ _____, in Britain most of the paths ___ ___ _____ ___ ___ _____, which can _____ __ ___ ___ _____. After the _____ _____—there's one bike that costs four thousand pounds but you can get a very good one for two hundred pounds—it's a cost-_____ _____. And there are _____ ___ ___, such as the Pyrenees Traverse, which has _____ _____ _____ ___ with no _____ _____.

Interviewer: _____ _____ my _____ _____—any advice on that?

Stan: Yes, swimming _____ _____ ___ __ _____ ___ _____. _____, for most people, the idea of being underwater, _____ ___ _____ _____, is a _____ one, but with good _____ you can pick it up in no time ___ _____. Once you ___ ___ _____ you _____ __ ___ _____ __ competent diver, you can do it anywhere.

Interviewer: I see you've got _____ ___ _____ ___. _____ that's only for people who are very _____ or _____?

Stan: Well, it is the sort of thing you'd _____ ___ _____ ___ in the movies, but you'd be _____ how many people go in for it these days. Six hours of training will give you _____ _____ ___ _____ _____ _____ _____. People who really take to it often _____ _____ _____, so if you _____ ___ ___, you might find yourself _____ ___ __ _____ _____.

Interviewer: OK, and finally, _____. That always looks ___ ___ _____ ___ ___—in that ___ boat with _____ _____ everywhere.

Stan: Well, there are some _____ ___ ___ water where the real canoeing _____ ___, _____ _____ can _____ __ _____ _____ and _____ ___. There's one _____ in Wales that _____ _____ for the _____ _____ that has a _____ _____, so that at _____ ___ ___ water runs through. You can _____ ___ and they'll say it's a ___ _____ tomorrow or a _____ _____, so you can choose your times _____ ___ _____.

Interviewer: OK, Stan, thanks a lot. After the break, we'll be going to Canada…

◎ 听力原文

Interviewer: ...Welcome back to the programme. Well, statistics show that the fastest-growing sports in Britain are adventure sports, and I have with me Stan Leach, an official at the Sports Council, who's going to tell us a bit about some of them. Stan, where shall we start?

Stan: Well, most people start with walking, I think—although of course strictly speaking it's not necessarily an adventure sport, but it's what gets most people outdoors. Indeed, the great thing about walking in Britain is the endless variety, from an easy stroll to a country pub, to an energetic walk up a high peak. If you want to take up walking, you can start with a few short circular walks and then pick something longer and more demanding.

Interviewer: What's this thing called scrambling I've been hearing about?

Stan: Yeah, scrambling is sort of in the grey area between walking and climbing. Scrambles are graded according to difficulty, and on the harder ones, which are quite close to rock climbing. It's best to go with an expert.

Interviewer: Well, that brings us nicely on to climbing—that's really caught on here lately, hasn't it?

Stan: Yes, and of course you know it doesn't have to mean going up the really big ones like Mount Qomolangma. Climbing might seem rather terrifying to begin with, but it's great fun and really keeps you fit. You start by climbing small crags before moving on to a rock face. I went for a day's lesson with mountaineer Alan Kimber in Scotland and it was really scary but really exciting.

Interviewer: Right, well, what's next?

Stan: Mountain biking. If you can get used to the saddle, you can cycle across Britain. But unlike in the USA, where there are special cycling paths, in Britain most of the paths are the same as for walkers, which can cause a bit of trouble. After the initial investment—there's one bike that costs four thousand pounds but you can get a very good one for two hundred pounds—it's a cost-efficient sport. And there are relatively easy trips, such as the Pyrenees Traverse, which has seventy percent downhill slopes with no major climbs.

Interviewer: Scuba diving's my personal favourite—any advice on that?

Stan: Yes, swimming underwater opens up a whole new world. Actually, for most people, the idea of being underwater, unable to breathe normally, is a frightening one, but with good tuition you can pick it up in no time at all. Once you get the qualification you need to be considered a competent diver, you can do it anywhere.

Interviewer: I see you've got skydiving on your list. Surely that's only for people who are very brave or mad?

Stan: Well, it is the sort of thing you'd expect to only see in the movies, but you'd be amazed how many people go in for it these days. Six hours of training will give you enough background to make the first jump. People who really take to it often join display teams, so if you take it up, you might find yourself taking part in special events.

Interviewer: OK, and finally, canoeing. That always looks a bit dangerous to me—in that tiny boat with water rushing everywhere.

Stan: Well, there are some terrible bits of water where the real canoeing experts go, but beginners can start in gentle waters and build up. There's one stretch in Wales that was designed for the world championships that has a dam release, so that at pre-set times the water runs through. You can phone up and they'll say it's a full release tomorrow or a quarter release, so you can choose your times according to difficulty.

Interviewer: OK, Stan, thanks a lot. After the break, we'll be going to Canada…

SECTION 2

▶ 听力原题

Part 4

You will hear a radio interview about a mountain-climbing weekend. For Questions 24–30, choose the best answer (A, B or C).

24 How did Douglas feel when he booked the weekend?

A. sure that he was ready to join the training

B. uncertain if it was a good idea for him

C. surprised that such activities were organised

25 Douglas expected that the experience would help him to

A. meet people with similar interests.

B. improve his mental capability.

C. discover his psychological limits.

26 He was surprised that the other participants

A. were there for reasons like his.

B. were experienced climbers.

C. were in better states than he was.

27 What did one of his friends say to him?

A. He was making a mistake.

B. Climbing was fashionable.

C. She was more proficient than him.

28 What did the people plan at the end of the trip?

A. to exchange cards

B. to take a different sort of trip together

C. to go on another climbing trip together

29 In what way did Douglas change as a result of the trip?

A. He took a greater interest in people.

B. He became more ambitious.

C. He began to notice more things around him.

30　Douglas's boots are still muddy because he wants them to

A. remind him of what he has achieved.

B. warn him not to do it again.

C. weaken his embarrassment.

▶ 填空练习

Interviewer: My guest today is Douglas Turner, who ＿＿＿ ＿＿ ＿ ＿＿ ＿＿＿ ＿ ＿＿＿＿ in Africa. Douglas, how did this come about?

Douglas: Well, I ＿＿＿ it ＿＿＿ ＿＿ ＿＿＿ ＿＿ ＿＿ ＿＿＿ holidays in the ＿＿＿ ＿＿ week after week; it somehow got into my ＿＿＿. Then there was one which said, 'Are you ready for the ＿＿＿ ＿＿＿ ＿＿＿ ＿ ＿＿ ＿＿? Five thousand metres. One weekend.' And somewhat ＿＿ ＿ ＿＿＿ ＿＿＿, I found myself ＿＿＿ ＿ ＿ ＿＿ ＿＿＿ ＿＿. You see, I simply ＿＿ ＿＿ for it; the nearest I'd got was a bit of ＿＿＿ five years ago.

Interviewer: What did you think you would get ＿＿ ＿ ＿ ＿＿＿?

Douglas: ＿＿＿ when I go to things, l enjoy ＿＿＿ ＿＿, but in this ＿＿ l was ＿＿＿ ＿＿ ＿＿ ＿＿ group would be ＿＿ ＿＿＿ ＿＿ ＿＿ ＿＿, and I wouldn't have ＿＿＿ ＿＿ ＿＿＿ ＿＿＿. And as for the ＿＿＿ ＿＿ ＿＿ ＿＿＿ ＿＿ ＿＿, I thought I'd be lucky if I ＿＿＿ ＿＿ ＿＿ at all! It was more ＿＿ ＿＿ ＿＿ ＿＿＿ ＿＿ ＿＿ what I was ＿＿＿ ＿＿ ＿＿ ＿＿. Would I get cold feet and not go at all? Or go, but ＿＿ ＿ ＿＿ ＿＿? That sort of thing.

Interviewer: But you made it to the top.

Douglas: Yes, I did. ＿＿＿ ＿ ＿＿ ＿＿, I can tell you.

Interviewer: And were you right about the other people?

Douglas: No, actually. There were a few ＿＿＿ ＿＿＿ and ＿＿＿, but most of the ＿＿＿ ＿＿ ＿＿＿ people who wanted to do something ＿＿ ＿＿＿ once in a while, ＿＿ ＿ ＿＿ like me, in fact. So not ＿＿＿ ＿＿ ＿＿. Though I have to ＿＿＿ ＿ nearly all of them were ＿＿＿ ＿＿ ＿. Actually, I hadn't realised so many people did this ＿＿ ＿ ＿＿＿. It was funny—when I told a friend that I was going, she said, 'Oh, not another one. Everyone I know's going ＿＿＿ ＿＿ ＿＿. There's a big thing about ＿＿＿ ＿＿ ＿＿＿ ＿＿＿ ＿＿ ＿ ＿＿, isn't there? You're welcome to it,' she said, 'You won't ＿＿＿ ＿ ＿ there.'

Interviewer: How did you all ____ ____ _____?

Douglas: I suppose we were a bit _____ __ each other at first, but that soon went, and we somehow _____ a _____ _____ _____ _____, and nobody _____ ____ _____ __ _____ ____ the slow ones, which usually _____ me. Or at least, if they did _____, they did it ____ __ _____. In fact, on the _____ home, we were _____ _____ ____, and _____ __ _____ another _____ ___ as a party— but without a mountain in sight this time.

Interviewer: So how did the weekend _____ ____ _____ _____?

Douglas: It was much better than I'd expected. It made me _____ ___ _____ _____. As I'd hoped, I _____ ___ _____, and I learnt to ____ __ ____ people I couldn't ____ _____, but I also became much _____ _____, of the ____ _____ ___ _____, for instance, and that was _____ __ _____.

Interviewer: I suppose you're going to be a _____ _____ _____ now.

Douglas: The pair of boots I wore I'm _____ ___ ___ ____still on them on my desk at work. They're a kind of _____, to _____ to myself that I've done it. But I somehow _____ ____ ____ __ _____ them again. I'm going to have to put them somewhere _____ _____, though, because it's sometimes a bit _____ when other people ___ _____.

Interviewer: Douglas Turner, thank you very much.

Douglas: Thank you.

▶ 听力原文

Interviewer: My guest today is Douglas Turner, who recently spent a weekend climbing a mountain in Africa. Douglas, how did this come about?

Douglas: Well, I suppose it started with seeing adverts for activity holidays in the national press week after week; it somehow got into my subconscious. Then there was one which said, 'Are you ready for the greatest physical challenge of your life? Five thousand metres. One weekend.' And somewhat against my better judgement, I found myself picking up the phone straight away. You see, I simply hadn't trained for it; the nearest I'd got was a bit of hill-walking five years ago.

Interviewer: What did you think you would get out of the weekend?

Douglas: Generally when I go to things, l enjoy meeting people, but in this case l was afraid the rest of the group would be a bunch of healthy types, and I wouldn't have much in common with them. And as for the physical effort of climbing the mountain, I thought I'd be lucky if I survived the weekend at all! It was more a kind of wanting to see what I was mentally capable of doing. Would I get cold feet and not go at all? Or go, but give up halfway up? That sort of thing.

Interviewer: But you made it to the top.

Douglas: Yes, I did. Much to my surprise, I can tell you.

Interviewer: And were you right about the other people?

Douglas: No, actually. There were a few serious walkers and climbers, but most of the participants were professional people who wanted to do something quite different once in a while, more or less like me, in fact. So not intimidating after all. Though I have to admit that nearly all of them were fitter than me. Actually, I hadn't realised so many people did this sort of thing. It was funny—when I told a friend that I was going, she said, 'Oh, not another one. Everyone I know's going climbing this year. There's a big thing about pushing yourself to your limit at the moment, isn't there? You're welcome to it,' she said, 'You won't catch me up there.'

Interviewer: How did you all get on together?

Douglas: I suppose we were a bit suspicious of each other at first, but that soon went, and we somehow developed a really close group feeling, and nobody complained about having to wait for the slow ones, which usually included me. Or at least, if they did complain, they did it out of earshot. In fact, on the flight home, we were busy exchanging cards, and decided to book another weekend trip as a party—but without a mountain in sight this time.

Interviewer: So how did the weekend compare with your expectations?

Douglas: It was much better than I'd expected. It made me change in subtle ways. As I'd hoped, I gained in self-knowledge, and I learnt to get on with people I couldn't escape from, but I also became much more observant, of the tiny little wild flowers, for instance, and that was quite a bonus.

Interviewer: I suppose you're going to be a regular mountain climber now.

Douglas: The pair of boots I wore I'm keeping with the mud still on them on my desk at work. They're a kind of trophy, to prove to myself that I've done it. But I somehow don't think I'll be using them again. I'm going to have to put them somewhere less visible, though, because it's sometimes a bit embarrassing when other people are impressed.

Interviewer: Douglas Turner, thank you very much.

Douglas: Thank you.

SECTION 3

▶ 听力原题

Part 4

You will hear part of a radio interview with Martin Middleton, who makes wildlife programmes for television. For Questions 24–30, choose the best answer (A, B or C).

24   What was the origin of Martin Middleton's love of travel?

A. meeting someone who'd been to Singapore

B. something he read as a child

C. a television film about Africa

25   When he visited Borneo, Martin

A. had no fixed expectations.

B. made a four months programme.

C. became more interested in filming old buildings.

26   Since the early 1960s, wildlife filming has become

A. more dynamic.

B. more creative.

C. more organised.

27   Looking back, Martin regards his experience on the iceberg as

A. slightly ridiculous.

B. extremely dangerous.

C. unusually sad.

28   When he takes a holiday, Martin prefers to

A. enjoy a sunbath by the sea.

B. stay in comfortable surroundings.

C. travel for a particular reason.

29   Martin thought that the holiday-makers he saw in the Dominican Republic were

A. doing harm to the environment.

B. wasting opportunities.

C. lacking entertainment.

30 What is Martin's opinion of tourism?

    A. It should not be encouraged.

    B. It can be a good thing.

    C. It is well managed.

▶ 填空练习

Interviewer: Today's guest _____ _____ _____. He is a man who has given us hours of _____ and _____ over the years, with his _____ _____ ___ _____ programmes. He is, of course, Martin Middleton. Martin, you've been to the four _____ ___ ____ _____ ___ _____ ___ _____. Where did this _____ ___ _____ _____ _____?

Martin: I don't really know…I didn't travel much as a child, but I _____ _____ about the *East* and _____ _____ ___ it. Then, when I was about twelve, I met someone who'd ____ __ _____—and to me that _____ _____…and, of course, when I _____ ___ _____, back in the early nineteen sixties, you didn't travel to make a wildlife programme…you _____ _____ and _____ ___ ____ _____ ___. So, when I said I'd like to go and film in Africa, the Head of Programmes just laughed at me.

Interviewer: And did you go to Africa?

Martin: _____ ____ _____, no! But I _____ __ _____ ___ _____ ____ to go to Borneo, in nineteen sixty-two. There was just me and a _____. We _____ _____ ___ four months, _____ _____ we found something interesting. We _____ __ _____, _____ up-river for ten days and _____ ___ __ ___ _____ _____. Nowadays, of course, it's all _____ _____.

Interviewer: Different? In what way?

Martin: We do _____ ____ _____ before we ____ _____, so when we _____ _____, we know _____ ____ _____ we want to get. I mean, you don't ____ ___ ____ the morning and say to your team, 'What shall we do this morning?' You have to _____ _____ _____ _____ ___ _____ ___ _____…to work to a _____ _____.

Interviewer: Some of your programmes _____ _____ _____ in some _____ _____ _____. It's hard to _____ other programme-makers wanting to ____ __ _____ or _____ that you've _____.

Martin: Well, if you want _____ _____, you've got to ____ ____ ____ _____ ____...but

you can ____ _____ doing some _____ _____ _____...um...like, for example, on

one occasion, _____ ___ ___ ___ _____ ___ ___ _____. There I was... _____

___. Then it _____ ___ _____, and the helicopter ____ _____ ____ __ ____ _____

and couldn't _____ ____ again. So I was _____ there, on this iceberg, thinking, 'This is

crazy... I didn't even want to come here!'

Interviewer: What I wonder is...where does somebody like yourself, who travels to all these _____

_____ as part of their work, go on holiday?

Martin: (laughs) I'm not very _____ ___ _____ ___ ___ _____, that's for sure. I wouldn't

go to a place just to sit around. It's nice to _____ ___ _____ when you're travelling...

to have something you want to film...um... I've just _____ _____ _____ the Dominican

Republic, and we were _____ ___ ____ ___ _____ night in a big hotel. The place was

_____ ____ ___ _____, just lying there, _____. They seemed quite happy

to spend the whole day _____ out around the pool...They never _____ to want to

go and _____ ___ _____ things there were to see _____ ___ _____. For me,

that would be a very _____ ___ to spend a holiday.

Interviewer: Your programmes, though, must _____ _____ __ ___ ___ _____ to take their

holidays in _____ and _____ places.

Martin: You are probably right, but...well...I _____ _____ _____ _____ ___ _____.

I go back to the places where, years ago, I was the only _____, and now there are

_____ ____ _____ three times a day. So you _____ ____ in ten years or so every

remote place on the _____ ____ ___ _____ ___, because everyone will be

_____ it. But, on the other hand, I am ___ _____ ___ ___ _____ that ____

_____ ___ _____ that _____ ___ _____. You can see a good

_____ of this in the Galapagos Islands, where the tourism is _____ _____.

That's very _____, and could be _____ _____ for the future...

▶ 听力原文

Interviewer: Today's guest needs no introduction. He is a man who has given us hours of interest and

entertainment over the years, with his weekly series of wildlife programmes. He is, of

course, Martin Middleton. Martin, you've been to the four corners of the earth in search of

material. Where did this love of adventures come from?

Martin: I don't really know…I didn't travel much as a child, but I remember reading about the *East* and being fascinated by it. Then, when I was about twelve, I met someone who'd been to Singapore—and to me that seemed incredible…and, of course, when I started in television, back in the early nineteen sixties, you didn't travel to make a wildlife programme…you went along and filmed at the local zoo. So, when I said I'd like to go and film in Africa, the Head of Programmes just laughed at me.

Interviewer: And did you go to Africa?

Martin: On that occasion, no! But I eventually got them to allow me to go to Borneo, in nineteen sixty-two. There was just me and a cameraman. We went off for four months, filming wherever we found something interesting. We bought a canoe, sailed up-river for ten days and ended up in a traditional longhouse. Nowadays, of course, it's all quite different.

Interviewer: Different? In what way?

Martin: We do months of preparation before we set off, so when we start filming, we know exactly what scenes we want to get. I mean, you don't get up in the morning and say to your team, 'What shall we do this morning?' You have to know exactly what each scene is going to show…to work to a strict plan.

Interviewer: Some of your programmes have taken place in some pretty remote areas. It's hard to imagine other programme-makers wanting to risk the dangerous or discomfort that you've experienced.

Martin: Well, if you want original material, you've got to go off the beaten track…but you can find yourself doing some pretty strange things…um…like, for example, on one occasion, jumping out of a helicopter onto an iceberg. There I was…freezing cold. Then it started to snow, and the helicopter had gone back to the ship and couldn't take off again. So I was stuck there, on this iceberg, thinking, 'This is crazy…I didn't even want to come here!'

Interviewer: What I wonder is…where does somebody like yourself, who travels to all these exotic places as part of their work, go on holiday?

Martin: (laughs) I'm not very good at lying on a beach, that's for sure. I wouldn't go to a place just to sit around. It's nice to have an objective when you're travelling…to have something you want to film…um…I've just come back from the Dominican Republic, and we were put up for the first night in a big hotel. The place was absolutely full of people, just lying there, sunbathing. They seemed quite happy to spend the whole day stretched out around the pool…They never seemed to want to go and explore the amazing things there were to see outside the hotel. For me, that would be a very boring way to spend a holiday.

Interviewer: Your programmes, though, must have inspired a lot of people to take their holidays in remote and little-known places.

Martin: You are probably right, but…well…I have mixed feelings about all this. I go back to the places where, years ago, I was the only European, and now there are cruise ships coming three times a day. So you worry that in ten years or so every remote place on the planet will be swallowed up, because everyone will be visiting it. But, on the other hand, I am in favour of tourism that is done in a way that protects the environment. You can see a good example of this in the Galapagos Islands, where the tourism is carefully managed. That's very successful, and could be a model for the future…

SECTION 4

▶ 听力原题

Part 4

You will hear part of a radio interview with Steve Thomas, a young chef who has his own cookery series on television. For Questions 24–30, choose the best answer (A, B or C).

24　On his TV programme, Steve likes to show audiences

　　A. the process of cooking.

　　B. tips to keep food from getting burn.

　　C. attractively presented dishes.

25　Steve was given his own TV series because

　　A. he cooked for a TV company.

　　B. he appeared on a TV programme.

　　C. he was referred to a TV producer.

26　What made him take up cooking as a child?

　　A. His parents expected him to cook in their restaurant.

　　B. He felt it was the best way of getting some money.

　　C. His father wanted to teach him to cook.

27　How did Steve feel once he got to college?

　　A. He has no interest in academics.

　　B. He regretted not studying harder at school.

　　C. He was confident about his practical work.

28　What does Steve say about the cooks who work for him?

　　A. He frequently raises his voice at them.

　　B. He demands a lot from them.

　　C. He trains them all himself.

29　Steve admires Ron Bell because

　　A. he prepares old fashioned dishes.

　　B. he writes excellent articles about food.

　　C. he makes a point of using local produce.

30 How will Steve's book be different from other books about cooking?

   A. the pictures that are attractive.

   B. the way that it is illustrated.

   C. the sort of person it is aimed at.

▶ 填空练习

Interviewer: With us today is Steve Thomas, a twenty-three-year-old chef who _____ _____ _____ ____ ____ _____ _____ programme. Steve, what's the _____ ___ _____ _____?

Steve: Well, I think I'm _____ ____ ____ TV _____ ___ _____ I want people to see how I _____ __ _____ ____ __ _____ go, so I don't _____ ___ ___ __ _____ that's half _____ already. If anything _____ __ _____ _____ the programme, you know, _____ something ____ _____, well, that's part of the _____. When they ____ _____ it themselves, then they'll see the _____ ___ __ _____ _____, but not on the screen.

Interviewer: So how did you come to _____ _____ ___ ___ _____?

Steve: I was _____ ___ __ _____ ____ the Gala in December last year when they came to ____ __ _____ ____ ____ place. I didn't even ____ __ ____ _____. I was ___ _____ _____ ____ and _____ ___. But the _____ ____ ___ and the _____ ___ ____ _____ __ __ _____ me a job…The Gala owner wished me all the best and let me go _____ __ _____.

Interviewer: Wow! Now, is it true that you _____ ____ __ _____ __ _____?

Steve: Well, you could say that…I _____ _____ __ ____ __ ___ ____. My Mum and Dad ____ __ _____, and Dad ____ __ ___ ___ __ _____ ____ then. My Mum was too busy _____ ____ ___…Dad _____ that if I wanted some money, I should _____ ____ it, and it seemed a lot _____ _____ to ____ ____ in the kitchen and see how things were made than to _____ my money _____ Dad's car…

Interviewer: You _____ __ _____ _____ at college. How did you like that?

Steve: At school I wasn't very good at anything much. At that time, my mind wasn't on _____ ____ ____ _____. I found sitting in a classroom, _____ ___ ____ _____ ___ _____, very, very trying. I _____ ___ ____ ___ college though and there I was fine, because when it came to the _____ _____, I knew what I was doing. I realised that a bit of _____ ____ _____ ____ you any ____ either and I found it ____ _____ when I was _____ ___ ___ _____, and so I've ___ _____ really.

Interviewer: And now you have a TV programme and several cooks _____ _____ _____ _____. How do you ___ ___ _____ them?

Steve: Oh, I love working with them. But on my programme everyone has to be _____ _____. They _____ ___ _____ _____ _____ _____ _____ _____ before they even _____ ____ the job. I _____ __ _____ __ ___ ___ ___ _____ I ____ __ _____ __ _ _____ if they ____ work _____, but I'm just as likely to _____ ___ if they do well. What I say to them is, you want the _____ __ ____ ___ ___ ___ _____, so we need to make a _____ _____…

Interviewer: Is there any _____ _____ that you _____ _____?

Steve: I _____ think that Ron Bell is the best, and I'm _____ that he's now got him his own food _____ in a newspaper. I had the _____ _____ of _____ with him ____ ___ _____. What's so _____ ___ ___ __ _____ he's always been _____ _____ _____ _____ that _____ ____ the area where he works…For example, the fish of the day _____ ___ ___ _____ from the river _____ ___ his _____. He's been _____ __ _____ to _____ _____, maybe that's a _____, but I think that's his _____.

Interviewer: I heard that you are also_____ ___ _____ __ _____.

Steve: Yes, I'm writing it ___ ____ _____. It may _____ _____ who ____ a lot of _____ _____, as most _____ nowadays seem to be things to ____ __ _____ ___ _____…I've ____ __ __ _____ that ____ __ ____ _____, with _____ _____ but it will be _____ _____ for most _____ __ _____. What I say in my book is that we must _____ ___ _____ __ __ ____ does not _____ ___ how it looks…it's what it _____ ____ and the _____ of the friends you'll share it ____ ____ _____.

Interviewer:　Well, thank you, Steve. I _____ _____ ___ _____ some _____...

▶ 听力原文

Interviewer:　With us today is Steve Thomas, a twenty-three-year-old chef who delights TV audiences with his imaginative cooking programme. Steve, what's the secret of your success?

Steve:　Well, I think I'm different from other TV chefs in that I want people to see how I prepare a dish from the word go, so I don't present them with a dish that's half prepared already. If anything should go wrong during the programme, you know, suppose something gets burned, well, that's part of the experience. When they try preparing it themselves, then they'll see the beauty of the finished product, but not on the screen.

Interviewer:　So how did you come to get your own TV series?

Steve:　I was working in a restaurant called the Gala in December last year when they came to make a documentary about the place. I didn't even look at the camera. I was too busy making pasta and cooking fish. But the producer spotted me and the following week they phoned me to offer me a job...The Gala owner wished me all the best and let me go without a complaint.

Interviewer:　Wow! Now, is it true that you come from a family of cooks?

Steve:　Well, you could say that...I started cooking at the age of eight. My Mum and Dad have a restaurant, and Dad used to do all the cooking back then. My Mum was too busy looking after us...Dad insisted that if I wanted some money, I should work for it, and it seemed a lot more interesting to help out in the kitchen and see how things were made than to earn my money washing Dad's car...

Interviewer:　You attended a catering course at college. How did you like that?

Steve:　At school I wasn't very good at anything much. At that time, my mind wasn't on anything other than cooking. I found sitting in a classroom, trying to pay attention to things, very, very trying. I managed to get to college though and there I was fine, because when it came to the actual cooking, I knew what I was doing. I realised that a bit of academic work didn't do you any harm either and I found it much easier when I was interested in the subject, and so I've no regrets really.

Interviewer:　And now you have a TV programme and several cooks working under your orders. How do you get on with them?

Steve: Oh, I love working with them. But on my programme everyone has to be really special. They need to have gone through college training before they even apply for the job. I suppose the problem is that fairly frequently I tend to raise my voice if they don't work efficiently, but I'm just as likely to praise them if they do well. What I say to them is, you want the audience to say we are the best, so we need to make a special effort…

Interviewer: Is there any chef celebrity that you admire especially?

Steve: I definitely think that Ron Bell is the best, and I'm pleased that he's now got him his own food column in a newspaper. I had the great privilege of working with him for a while. What's so special about him is that he's always been enthusiastic about using ingredients that come from the area where he works…For example, the fish of the day would be the catch from the river close to his restaurant. He's been criticised for sticking to old-fashioned recipes, maybe that's a weakness, but I think that's his decision.

Interviewer: I heard that you are also going to write a book.

Steve: Yes, I'm writing it at the moment. It may disappoint readers who expect a lot of glossy pictures, as most cookbooks nowadays seem to be things to look at rather than read…I've gone for a style that may be less attractive, with fewer colour pictures but it will be more useful for most types of reader. What I say in my book is that we must remember the success of a meal does not depend on how it looks…it's what it tastes like and the company of the friends you'll share it with that matters.

Interviewer: Well, thank you, Steve. I look forward to trying some recipes…

FCE 听力原题答案

FCE LISTENING

FCE LISTENING

FCE LISTENING

FCE LISTENING

FCE LISTENING

FCE LISTENING

FCE LISTENING

FCE LISTENING

FCE LISTENING

FCE LISTENING

CHAPTER 1   FCE LISTENING PART 1

SECTION 1

| 1. C | 2. B | 3. B | 4. C | 5. C | 6. B | 7. A | 8. A |

SECTION 2

| 1. A | 2. C | 3. B | 4. B | 5. C | 6. A | 7. A | 8. A |

SECTION 3

| 1. B | 2. B | 3. C | 4. A | 5. A | 6. C | 7. B | 8. A |

SECTION 4

| 1. A | 2. A | 3. B | 4. C | 5. B | 6. A | 7. A | 8. C |

CHAPTER 2   FCE LISTENING PART 2

SECTION 1

9. tunnels	10. space (and) fresh air	11. Wales	12. climbing
13. (hard) hat	14. lamp	15. (strong) boots	16. all ages
17. special interest	18. competitions		

SECTION 2

9. travel agency	10. *High Adventure*	11. mending/repairing	12. 6 days
13. local	14. bored	15. (enormous) storms	16. (World) Sailing Club
17. (other) ships	18. diaries		

SECTION 3

9. British Airways/BA	10. cabin	11. motorbike	12. Australia
13. helpers	14. fuel	15. 9 months	16. sea
17. accurate	18. tired		

SECTION 4

9. German (and) Spanish	10. (tour) guide	11. World Travel	12. 4 months
13. advertising	14. journalists	15. adventure holidays	16. hometown
17. presenter	18. conference		

CHAPTER 3　FCE LISTENING PART 3

SECTION 1

19. C　　　20. D　　　21. B　　　22. F　　　23. A

SECTION 2

19. D　　　20. C　　　21. F　　　22. B　　　23. A

SECTION 3

19. D　　　20. F　　　21. E　　　22. A　　　23. C

SECTION 4

19. C　　　20. D　　　21. F　　　22. B　　　23. A

CHAPTER 4　FCE LISTENING PART 4

SECTION 1

24. B　　25. A　　26. C　　27. A　　28. B　　29. A　　30. A

SECTION 2

24. B　　25. C　　26. A　　27. B　　28. B　　29. C　　30. A

SECTION 3

24. B　　25. A　　26. C　　27. A　　28. C　　29. B　　30. B

SECTION 4

24. A　　25. B　　26. B　　27. C　　28. B　　29. C　　30. B

扫描二维码

输入封面防伪标涂层下的序列号

在线收听本书音频

图书在版编目（CIP）数据

FCE听力从突破到跨越.Ⅰ／王宏编著. --2版

北京：中国人民大学出版社，2025.6 --ISBN 978-7

-300-33909-2

Ⅰ. H319.9

中国国家版本馆CIP数据核字第2025BU8439号

- 本书中所有理论、概念均系作者原创，如果引用需注明出处。
- 本书著作权归作者所有，出版权归中国人民大学出版社，任何复印、引用均需征求著作权人及出版权持有人同时同意。

FCE听力从突破到跨越（第二版）（Ⅰ）

王宏　编著

FCE Tingli cong Tupo dao Kuayue (Di-er Ban) (Ⅰ)

出版发行	中国人民大学出版社	
社　　址	北京中关村大街31号	**邮政编码**　100080
电　　话	010-62511242（总编室）	010-62511770（质管部）
	010-82501766（邮购部）	010-62514148（门市部）
	010-62511173（发行公司）	010-62515275（盗版举报）
网　　址	http://www.crup.com.cn	
经　　销	新华书店	
印　　刷	唐山玺诚印务有限公司	
开　　本	787mm×1092mm　1/16	**版　　次**　2021年1月第1版
		2025年6月第2版
印　　张	6.25	**印　　次**　2025年9月第2次印刷
字　　数	74 000	**定　　价**　39.80元（全两册）

FCE听力
从突破到跨越

（第二版）

（II）

王宏 编著

中国人民大学出版社
· 北京 ·

目 录
CONTENTS

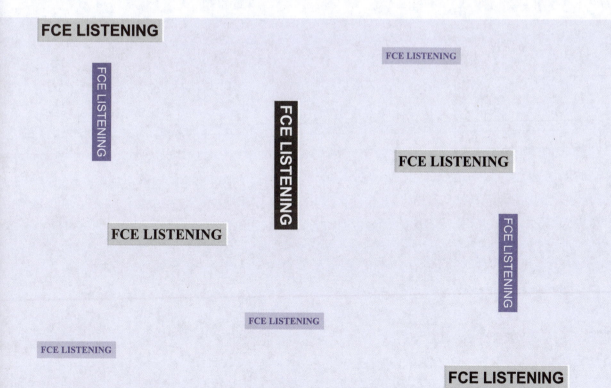

SECTION 1

◑ 听力原题

Part 1

You will hear people talking in eight different situations. For Questions 1–8, choose the best answer (A, B or C).

___

1 You hear a restaurant manager talking about the cooks who work for him.

   What does he say about them?

   A. They dislike cleaning pots and pans.

   B. They have a choice of jobs.

   C. They help to decide the menu.

2 You hear a woman talking about a new book.

   What does she particularly like about the book?

   A. It provides a lot of information.

   B. It is well-organised.

   C. It is enjoyable.

3 You hear the writer of a television soap opera being interviewed about the programme.

   What will happen next in the story?

   A. Someone will accept an important decision.

   B. Someone will go away unexpectedly.

   C. Someone will learn the truth at last.

4 You hear part of a radio interview.

   Who is speaking?

   A. a taxi driver

   B. a porter

   C. a passenger

5 You hear a woman talking about how she keeps fit.

   Why did she decide to take up line dancing?

   A. She thought the pace would suit her.

   B. She learned it from a television programme.

   C. She wanted to try exercising to music.

6   You overhear a conversation in a restaurant.

What does the woman think about the food she has just eaten?

A. It was expensive.

B. It was delicious.

C. It appeared to be fine.

7   You turn on the radio and hear a man talking.

What is he talking about?

A. drawing design drafts

B. writing fiction

C. composing music

8   You overhear a student phoning her parents.

What is her opinion of the place she is living in while at college?

A. She is not sure she will have enough room to study.

B. Her room is too tiny to fit all her stuff.

C. She does not get on well with her room-mates.

▶ 填空练习

Question 1

As a restaurant manager, I feel _____ ____ ____ _____ ___ the food we serve. So it's ___ ___ ___ ___ _____ ___ _____ that have been _____ _____ to _____ _____ they are of _____ _____, and to _____ ___ _____ the day. The cooks _____ __ _____ ten a.m. to _____ _____ and I'll take them _____ _____ _____. Because lunch is _____ over a _____ _____ ___ time it can get very busy and very hot. But _____ _____ _____, we _____ __ _____ the jobs up _____ ___ who likes doing what, and that _____ _____ _____ and _____ and _____ _____ before dinner.

Question 2

It's a _____ _____, a _____ _____ _____ and it's _____. I mean it's _____ _____ and it's not going to _____ ___ __ _____ _____ ___ ____ good for school work. That's what's really nice about it. Here is a _____ ___ which it is fun to _____ ___ and ____ ___. It's _____ _____ ___ _____ anyone _____ __ _____ and it _____ _____ _____ to any school _____, unlike so much of what is _____ today. But for anyone who likes little_____, you know, you can _____ ___ ____ __ ___ _____, for example, and see what else happened then, it's a very good book.

Question 3

Man: So, there've been some _____ _____ in Victoria Street this past week, what with Mariela _____ ___ ___ _____ Jason, and Stephen leaving home in the _____ ___ a family ____. Are next week's _____ ____ _____?

Woman: Well, I can't give away the _____ _____, but I don't think you'll be _____! I can tell you that Stephen's mother is _____ to tell her husband the secret she's _____ _____ ___ _____, which _____ __ _____ _____ and ___ _____ _____. And Jason _____ ___ _____ Mariela's _____, so you're going to hear a lot more from him, and ____ ___ ___ ____ _____ there.

Question 4

We get people to the taxis, that's the first _____, and to the trains. We _____ _____ they _____ ___ _____ and ____ _____ _____. These days many passengers have a lot of _____ and they want _____ ____ it. So we _____ _____ _____. We even take people down to the Underground or to places in the _____ _____. But ___ _____ ___ ____ are _____ _____ with a lot of bags and perhaps _____ ___ _____ _____, young children and so on. _____ they can't _____ everything on their own.

Question 5

I exercise in the form of dance. At one time I did _____ because exercise is more interesting with music, but I've since _____ on to _____ _____. It's ____ _____, but I go three times a week. I ____ ___ ____ _____, work hard, and it's just a way to ____ ____ _____ _____ watch television. It's also a _____ _____ ___ ____ the new ____. I think young people sometimes _____ _____ too far, get _____ with how they look, when they'll never ___ _____ ___ _____ __ ____ at that sort of pace. _____ line dancing _____ ___ ___ _____ I could _____ ___ _____ ___ my _____ ___.

Question 6

Man: Well, what did you think of that, then?

Woman: Brilliant! I've never _____ _____ like it! I wish now I'd tried this place sooner. I mean, I've been _____ ____ it for years.

Man: Why didn't you?

5

Woman:　Well, __ ___ _____, I never thought I'd be able to _____ ___, but it's _____ _____ _____. Mind you, I think they could _____ _____ ___ _____ _____ _____ _____. I think if food looks good on the plate, you _____ _____ __ __ _____ good. Yours was okay, but I think they could _____ ____ _____ __ __ _____ ____ _____.

Question 7

In _____ _____, the place I'm in doesn't _____ __ _____, ___ _____ ___ I _____ ___ _____ _____, you know, pencil and paper and, of course, my keyboard. Once I'm started, I go over things again and again—_____ ___ __ _____ if anyone's listening. I _____ __ ____ _____ here and there, but _____ I tend to ____ ____ an idea once I have it. I guess home's the best place in a way because there I'm _____ _____ to ____ __ _____ _____, and that's what you need to do, ____ _____ __ _____ __ _____ ___ __...

Question 8

Well, I'm _____ ___ two other girls…I know, it was _____ __ __ ___ and one other person, but there's a _____ ___ _____, _____. Anyway, the room's rather _____, but it's great. There've been three parties so far, and it's still the first week. It's an _____ _____ _____, with doors _____ and people _____ and _____ till the small hours. Yes, I _____ we'll have to ____ _____ to work soon, though I don't know how we'll be able to, _____ ____ that _____ _____—none of us is _____ _____…

▶ 听力原文

Question 1

As a restaurant manager, I feel responsible for the quality of the food we serve. So it's up to me to check the ingredients that have been delivered overnight to make sure they are of sufficient quality, and to produce a menu for the day. The cooks arrive at about ten a.m. to prepare lunch and I'll take them through the menu. Because lunch is concentrated over a short period of time it can get very busy and very hot. But unlike some kitchens, we tend to divide the jobs up according to who likes doing what, and that includes cleaning pots and pans and clearing the place before dinner.

Question 2

It's a factual book, a chronicle of the twentieth century and it's wonderful. I mean it's terribly bitty and it's not going to give you a lot of information nor be good for school work. That's what's really nice about it. Here is a reference book which it is fun to dip in and out of. It's hardly going to help anyone write an essay and it avoids being geared to any school syllabus, unlike so much of what is published today. But for anyone who likes little details, you know, you can look up your date of birth, for example, and see what else happened then, it's a very good book.

Question 3

Man: So, there've been some dramatic events in Victoria Street this past week, what with Mariela deciding not to marry Jason, and Stephen leaving home in the middle of a family row. Are next week's episodes as exciting?

Woman: Well, I can't give away the whole story, but I don't think you'll be disappointed! I can tell you that Stephen's mother is forced to tell her husband the secret she's been hiding for years, which leads to more fireworks and a few tears. And Jason refuses to accept Mariela's decision, so you're going to hear a lot more from him, and look out for some surprises there.

Question 4

We get people to the taxis, that's the first priority, and to the trains. We make sure they get on early and get comfortable seats. These days many passengers have a lot of luggage and they want assistance with it. So we provide much-needed service. We even take people down to the Underground or to places in the surrounding streets. But the majority of users are airline passengers with a lot of bags and perhaps accompanied by elderly relatives, young children and so on. Obviously they can't manage everything on their own.

Question 5

I exercise in the form of dance. At one time I did aerobics because exercise is more interesting with music, but I've since moved on to line dancing. It's less energetic, but I go three times a week. I run my own business, work hard, and it's just a way to cut off rather than watch television. It's also a challenge keeping up with the new steps. I think young people sometimes take exercise too far, get over-concerned with how they look, when they'll never be able to keep it up at that sort of pace. Whereas line dancing struck me as something I could sustain as part of my normal life.

Question 6

Man: Well, what did you think of that, then?

Woman: Brilliant! I've never tasted anything like it! I wish now I'd tried this place sooner. I mean, I've been walking past it for years.

Man: Why didn't you?

Woman: Well, to be honest, I never thought I'd be able to afford it, but it's actually quite reasonable. Mind you, I think they could have tried a bit harder with the presentation. I think if food looks good on the plate, you automatically expect it to taste good. Yours was okay, but I think they could have made more of an effort with mine.

Question 7

In practical terms, the place I'm in doesn't matter too much, as long as I have the necessary tools, you know, pencil and paper and, of course, my keyboard. Once I'm started, I go over things again and again—must be very dull if anyone's listening. I change a few notes here and there, but basically I tend to stick with an idea once I have it. I guess home's the best place in a way because there I'm relaxed enough to let my imagination flow, and that's what you need to do, in order to produce a good piece…

Question 8

Well, I'm sharing with two other girls…I know, it was supposed to be me and one other person, but there's a shortage of accommodation, apparently. Anyway, the room's rather cramped, but it's great. There've been three parties so far, and it's still the first week. It's an incredibly noisy place, with doors banging and people laughing and shouting till the small hours. Yes, I suppose we'll have to get down to work soon, though I don't know how we'll be able to, packed into that little space—none of us is very tidy…

SECTION 2

▶ 听力原题

Part 1

You will hear people talking in eight different situations. For Questions 1–8, choose the best answer (A, B or C).

---

1   You overhear a woman talking to her husband on a mobile phone.

      What is the background to the conversation?

      A. The family's holiday may have to be cancelled.

      B. This woman wants her son to study some computer technologies.

      C. Their son has schoolwork to complete before the start of term.

2   You hear a phone-in programme on the radio.

      Why has the man phoned?

      A. to complain about the traffic scheme

      B. to express his support for the traffic scheme

      C. to doubt the targets of the traffic scheme

3   On the radio, you hear a woman talking about her house.

      What has she recently done?

      A. decided to move to another area

      B. solved a problem that she had

      C. asked someone to upgrade her house

4   You overhear two people discussing a friend.

      What language does their friend usually speak at home?

      A. French

      B. English

      C. Italian

5   You hear a man talking about an activity holiday he went on as a child with his family.

      How did he feel during the holiday?

      A. bored by the climbing

      B. upset with his father

      C. found boating unpleasant

6   You hear the beginning of a radio programme.

What is the programme going to be about?

A. the development of second childhood

B. the environment

C. a form of entertainment

7   You hear a man being interviewed about a new project he has set up.

What is the purpose of the project?

A. to help people find accommodation in Scotland

B. to aid people in finding accommodation in Australia

C. to advise people how to set up a flat agency

8   You switch on the radio in the middle of a programme.

What kind of programme is it?

A. an arts review

B. a news talk show

C. a quiz show

▶ 填空练习

Question 1

Listen, about Jimmy's school project. I spoke to the _____ _____ at work about _____ __ _____, and _____ they're only _____ ___ ____ ____ ____ to people on _____ _____. So I guess Jimmy will just have to write it all out ___ _____ and _____ ___ ____ when we ____ _____. That'll only give him two days, but what can we do? I know he's been at home all summer, but that's Jimmy for you, and he's only twelve. I just _____ ___ _____ was a bit _____ _____ about people's _____ _____.

Question 2

Woman: Go ahead, Paul, I'm listening.

Man: Well...I'm ____ __ ____ _____ __ all your _____ _____ __ about the new _____ _____. I mean, that woman who said it _____ _____ _____ __ _____ the city by car _____ __ ____ _____ _____. Poor thing! Why doesn't she leave the car at home and use the ____ _____ _____? Anyway, the aim of the new _____ isn't to _____ ____ _____ _____; it's for _____ and _____ and _____ and ____ _____, and it's working. I _____ _____ ___ _____ __ _____ in the city centre and see for themselves. That's all I wanted to say.

Question 3

I ____ _____ ____ ____ _____, I can't _____ it, but when you've lived in a house ____ ___
____ __ __ ____, you learn to ____ __ _____ and you ____ _____ ____ __ ____
____. Here, the garden is a bit ____ ___ me to ____ ___ __ __ _____ ____, but now I've got
someone who comes in once a week to ____ __ ____, and things ____ _____ _____, so I
think I'll be _____ __ ____ just a little ____ _____.

Question 4

Man: I had dinner at Mark's house last night. His father ____ __ _____ ____ _____.

Woman: Oh, yes, his parents are Italian, _____ ____? I keep _____ that because Mark's
English is so good.

Man: Of course it is! He ____ _____ __ _____. And his mother's not Italian, she's
_____. That's what they all ____ __ ____ _____, though they ____ English
when I was there. Mark has to go to classes on Saturdays to ____ __ ____ and write
Italian. To hear him speak on the phone to his grandmother in Rome, you'd think it was his
___ _____!

Question 5

As a child all our _____ were in Scotland because my father was ____ ____ __ _____ and he
_____ __ ____ _____ every day. One day the weather _____ us ____ _____, ____ ___
__ _____, so we ____ __ ____ ___ __ __ ____. My father _____ it was _____
and ____ (he _____ _____) but I ____ ____ and _____, 'This feels good!'—even though
the boat was old and _____. After that, I just got the ____ really...and I've ____ _____ ____
_____. And the boats now are ____ ___ ____ first one in Scotland!

Question 6

As any parent or _____ knows, it's _____ _____ ___ or _____ _____ for small
children; give them a ____ ____, a _____ __ and a _____ ___, and they'll ____ ____
___ ___ ____. So you could say that the _____ _____ Thump are _____ _____ ___
_____ _____. Just over seven years ago, this small band of ____ _____ from the ____
__ England _____ __ ___ their _____ __ ___ _____ ___ and ____ _____ ___ ___
_____ ____. They now have five _____ ____ _____ _____ _____ the country and are
just about to ____ ___ _____ ____ of the USA.

Question 7

Woman: Mark, this new project you've got, this _____ _____, has this _____ from your ____ _____, or what?

Man: Both from _____ _____ _____ ___ _____ to find somewhere to live in Edinburgh over the last few years—_____ ___ ___ _____ one corner to the next and _____ __ _____ __ _____ which weren't _____…and also it was _____ _____ __ ____ __ _____ where a _____ _____ ___ ___ ___ and I _____, 'Well, let's try and take out some of the _____ of trying to find a ____ here in Scotland.'

Question 8

Woman: And now, Mr Harman, what I want to ask you is ___ _____ of Shakespeare's _____ does the _____ Queen Titania _____?

Man: Mmm, now let me think ____ __ _____. Well, it was one of the _____. I believe she was a _____…

Woman: I can tell you that _____ ___ _____ at the Regent Theatre last year _____ Eveline Thomas and ____ _____ _____.

Man: I don't _____ ____. Now, is it *Midsummer Night's Dream*, by William Shakespeare?

Woman: _____ it is!

▶ 听力原文

Question 1

Listen, about Jimmy's school project. I spoke to the computer department at work about borrowing a laptop, and apparently they're only supposed to give them out to people on company business. So I guess Jimmy will just have to write it all out by hand and type it out when we get back. That'll only give him two days, but what can we do? I know he's been at home all summer, but that's Jimmy for you, and he's only twelve. I just wish his school was a bit more understanding about people's holiday arrangements.

Question 2

Woman: Go ahead, Paul, I'm listening.

Man: Well…I'm fed up with listening to all your callers moaning on about the new traffic scheme. I mean, that woman who said it took fifty minutes to cross the city by car instead of her usual thirty. Poor thing! Why doesn't she leave the car at home and use the bus service instead? Anyway, the aim of the new scheme isn't to make car journeys quicker; it's for shoppers and pedestrians and cyclists and bus passengers, and it's working. I recommend everyone to have a walk in the city centre and see for themselves. That's all I wanted to say.

Question 3

I do sometimes think about moving, I can't deny it, but when you've lived in a house for as long as I have, you learn to accept its drawbacks and you stop always trying to change things. Here, the garden is a bit big for me to cope with as I would like, but now I've got someone who comes in once a week to help me out, and things have definitely improved, so I think I'll be staying put for just a little bit longer.

Question 4

Man: I had dinner at Mark's house last night. His father made a delicious Italian dessert.

Woman: Oh, yes, his parents are Italian, aren't they? I keep forgetting that because Mark's English is so good.

Man: Of course it is! He was born in Texas. And his mother's not Italian, she's French. That's what they all speak to each other, though they used English when I was there. Mark has to go to classes on Saturdays to learn to read and write Italian. To hear him speak on the phone to his grandmother in Rome, you'd think it was his first language!

Question 5

As a child all our holidays were in Scotland because my father was very keen on climbing and he insisted we went climbing every day. One day the weather stopped us going climbing, much to my relief, so we hired a rowing boat on the lake. My father complained it was uncomfortable and slow (he preferred motorboats) but I sat there and thought, 'This feels good!'—even though the boat was old and creaky. After that, I just got the bug really…and I've been rowing ever since. And the boats now are better than that first one in Scotland!

Question 6

As any parent or childcarer knows, it's pointless buying drums or expensive instruments for small children; give them a wooden spoon, a saucepan lid and a cardboard box, and they'll happily bang away for hours. So you could say that the group named Thump are simply having their second childhood. Just over seven years ago, this small band of street performers from the north of England decided to turn their routine with metal rubbish bins and bicycle chains into a stage show. They now have five separate groups working nightly across the country and are just about to begin their first tour of the USA.

Question 7

Woman: Mark, this new project you've got, this flat agency, has this arisen from your own experience, or what?

Man: Both from bitter personal experience of having to find somewhere to live in Edinburgh over the last few years—crossing the city from one corner to the next and turning up at hundreds of places which weren't suitable…and also it was taken from an idea in Australia where a similar service was set up and I thought, 'Well, let's try and take out some of the misery of trying to find a flat here in Scotland.'

Question 8

Woman: And now, Mr Harman, what I want to ask you is in which of Shakespeare's plays does the character Queen Titania appear?

Man: Mmm, now let me think for a moment. Well, it was one of the comedies. I believe she was a fairy…

Woman: I can tell you that it was performed at the Regent Theatre last year starring Eveline Thomas and had excellent reviews.

Man: I don't remember that. Now, is it *Midsummer Night's Dream*, by William Shakespeare?

Woman: Indeed it is!

SECTION 3

▶ 听力原题

Part 1

You will hear people talking in eight different situations. For Questions 1–8, choose the best answer (A, B or C).

---

1   You hear some information about a country on a travel programme.

   Where do most people spend the summer months?

   A. on the beach

   B. in the capital city

   C. in the mountains

2   You hear part of a radio programme about chewing gum.

   What is the speaker doing?

   A. outlining its history

   B. describing the features of American gum

   C. explaining its popularity

3   You hear part of a radio programme where listeners phone in with their opinions.

   What does the man want to do?

   A. express his disappointment

   B. complain his overwhelming workload

   C. encourage other listeners

4   You hear a woman speaking on the radio about buying a painting for the first time.

   What opinion is she expressing?

   A. A painting can be a worthwhile investment.

   B. Choose paintings that suit your home.

   C. Take your time when buying your first painting.

5   You hear a man being interviewed on the radio.

   What does he say about his mother?

   A. She encouraged him to become an artist.

   B. She persuaded him to do research.

   C. She wanted him to make money.

6　You hear part of an interview with a woman who is talking about her day.

What is her profession?

A. a teacher

B. a doctor

C. a housewife

7　You hear a man talking on the radio about teaching beginners to surf in the sea.

What does the man say about beginners?

A. They are very sensitive to criticism.

B. They need to be given appropriate goals.

C. They need to keep the same pace.

8　You hear part of an interview with a crime novelist.

What point is he making about his novels?

A. They are based on real-life crimes.

B. They include accurate descriptions of life in the past.

C. They decrease the length according to the historical period.

▶ 填空练习

Question 1

In the _____ _____ _____, the weather in the capital city is _____ and the _____ ___ _____. If you're there then, the best thing to do is _____ ___ in a pool ____ ____ or _____ _____ _____ _____. You could, however, _____ _____ where it's cooler. The Citra Mountains _____ __ north-east _____ _____ _____ _____, but ___ _____ _____ ____ __ _____ ___ _____ __ _____ ____ ___ _____ capital, which is a pity, because the coast and the mountains are _____ _____.

Question 2

Although it's popular _____, _____ ___ is a _____ US _____, _____ during the _____ ___ ____ _____ in the 1860s. The _____ ___ _____ ___ _____ ___ _____ __ is the _____ gum, _____, _____ ____ the _____ _____ _____ in Central America. Recently, _____ _____ have come into _____ ___, and _____ ___ __ _____ gum now include a _____ _____ ____ and a gum filled with _____ _____. In the US alone, sales of chewing gum _____ ____ $800 million a year, and worldwide some several billion.

16

Question 3

Woman: Go ahead, David. What have you got to say?

Man: Well, I'm 55. I was a ____ _____ until ten years ago, and then I lost my job. I was angry, I can tell you. But you can't just ____ _____ _____ sorry for yourself, like most of _____ _____. Can I just say to anyone listening: my story will give you heart. A bank manager has to ___ __ _____ listener, right? So I thought, 'How can I use that skill?'—maybe I could be a _____ ___ some sort—you know, help people _____ _____ _____ _____ _____. I'm busier now than I've ever been!

Question 4

The first _____ _____ _____ __ _____ is to _____ __ ____ ___ _____ that this will make you _____ _____ to keep you in your ___ ____. The _____ _____ is that you must really like the work itself. Ask yourself, can you _____ __ on the wall next to the TV? Are you happy to have this painting as a _____ ___ _____ ____? With this _____ _____, you can now ____ _____ _____ ___ the art market. You should do your homework. Fine _____ _____ _____; visit a student _____; ____ _____ some _____ __ _____.

Question 5

My mother could see I was _____ and she would _____ ____ _____ ____ ____ ____, but she was _____ __ _____ that I would ____ _____ ___ ____, _____ I mean, as she _____ _____ _____. So she helped me with my science homework—she really _____ ___—if it _____ ____ ____ her, I wouldn't be where I am today. I feel deep down—I ___ _____ __ _____ _____ ____ ___ art, _____ ____ _____; I even won some _____ ___ my pictures...and I still _____ _____ __ ____. But I _____, when I was _____ ____, I didn't think I would ever ____ _____ ___ ____ _____, so I studied science at university, then _____ a few years in ____ _____ _____ _____ __ __ _____ in the _____ _____.

Question 6

My day starts at 6 o'clock—it's somewhat _____ ___ _____ _____ in the morning as we're all _____ _____! I try to _____ __ _____ _____ the animals, and then there's the twins to _____ _____ ____ school, and I get to the _____ __ _____ 8 a.m. There's always a lot of _____ to do. Then it's _____ _____ all day. We've got a _____ _____ us ____ ____ _____ for six months, so I spend some time with her, _____ ___ she's _____ _____ it all—I enjoy _____ ___ _____.

Question 7

When you _____ _____, __ ___ _____ you have to _____ a course for each of them—getting the _____ ____ for each day's _____ __ _____ —age or sex _____ _____ _____ ; it's _____. Some are _____ ___ they_____ __ ___ ____ _____ __ __ _____, or maybe _____ ___ ___ __ _____ _____ is enough. Most can learn to _____ ___ ___ __ _____ __ ____ because of the _____ _____ __ _____. Others just _____ _____ _____ _____ _____ _____ . Some make _____ _____ like _____ _____ ____ through the legs of their _____, but most _____ _____ _____ _____!

Question 8

Interviewer: Now John, you write around four _____ _____ _____ each year. How do you _____ ___?

John: Well, _____ ___ _____ and _____ themselves are _____ ____, I want my books to be _____ _____ ___ _____ _____ of everyday life I describe. And the further back in history you go, the _____ _____ _____ _____ . So, I'm _____ ___ _____ ___ ___ __ _____ _____ _____ , and then I'm _____ _____ ___ _____ _____ . And, let's face it. If a _____ _____ _____ ____ 80, 000 words to _____ ___ _____, he begins to look a bit _____, _____ he?

▶ 听力原文

Question 1

In the main summer months, the weather in the capital city is hot and the humidity is terrible. If you're there then, the best thing to do is either sit in a pool all day or surround yourself with air-conditioning. You could, however, head higher where it's cooler. The Citra Mountains behind the north-east coast have stunning scenery, but the majority never seem to make the effort to get out of the capital, which is a pity, because the coast and the mountains are much pleasanter.

Question 2

Although it's popular worldwide, chewing gum is a uniquely US product, discovered during the search for rubber materials in the 1860s. The basic raw material for all chewing gum is the natural gum, chicle, obtained from the sapodilla tree found in Central America. Recently, man-made substitutes have come into widespread use, and popular types of chewing gum now include a soft-chunk bubble gum and a gum filled with flavoured liquid. In the US alone, sales of chewing gum total over $800 million a year, and worldwide some several billion.

Question 3

Woman: Go ahead, David. What have you got to say?

Man: Well, I'm 55. I was a bank manager until ten years ago, and then I lost my job. I was angry, I can tell you. But you can't just sit about feeling sorry for yourself, like most of your callers. Can I just say to anyone listening: my story will give you heart. A bank manager has to be a good listener, right? So I thought, 'How can I use that skill?'—maybe I could be a counsellor of some sort—you know, help people deal with their personal problems. I'm busier now than I've ever been!

Question 4

The first rule about buying a painting is to immediately put aside any notion that this will make you enough money to keep you in your old age. The overriding factor is that you must really like the work itself. Ask yourself, can you imagine it on the wall next to the TV? Are you happy to have this painting as a fixture in your life? With this in mind, you can now set about looking into the art market. You should do your homework. Fine tune your taste; visit a student exhibition; flick through some contemporary art magazines.

Question 5

My mother could see I was artistic and she would never have stood in my way, but she was desperate to ensure that I would do well in life, financially I mean, as she had always struggled. So she helped me with my science homework—she really pushed me—if it hadn't been for her, I wouldn't be where I am today. I feel deep down—I do have a more natural talent for art, rather than science; I even won some awards for my pictures…and I still paint whenever I can. But I suppose, when I was growing up, I didn't think I would ever earn enough as an artist, so I studied science at university, then spent a few years in the States working as a researcher in the oil industry.

Question 6

My day starts at 6 o'clock—it's somewhat chaotic at home early in the morning as we're all rushing around! I try to help my husband feed the animals, and then there's the twins to get ready for school, and I get to the surgery at around 8 a.m. There's always a lot of paperwork to do. Then it's seeing patients all day. We've got a trainee watching us at the moment for six months, so I spend some time with her, making sure she's making sense of it all—I enjoy working with students.

Question 7

When you teach beginners, in a sense you have to tailor-make a course for each of them—getting the objectives right for each day's course is fundamental—age or sex makes little difference; it's attitude. Some are delighted if they manage to get their knees on a surfboard, or maybe standing up in the first session is enough. Most can learn to stand up in half a day because of the foamy boards we use. Others just keep going until they've succeeded. Some make daft mistakes like putting their arms through the legs of their wetsuits, but most beginners are quite sensible!

Question 8

Interviewer: Now John, you write around four historical crime novels each year. How do you manage it?

John: Well, although the characters and stories themselves are made up, I want my books to be historically correct in the details of everyday life I describe. And the further back in history you go, the fewer actual details survive. So, I'm careful to keep them to a similar length, and then I'm less tempted to invent things. And, let's face it. If a detective takes more than 80, 000 words to solve a crime, he begins to look a bit dim, doesn't he?

SECTION 4

▶ 听力原题

Part 1

You will hear people talking in eight different situations. For Questions 1–8, choose the best answer (A, B or C).

1   You hear someone talking about women's football.

What is she doing when she speaks?

A. encouraging young girls to support a team

B. suggesting how to attract young girls to the sport

C. Introducing the Women's World Cup and the Olympics.

2   You hear a man talking on the radio about a bag made for use on walking trips.

How does this new bag differ from others?

A. It has comfortable, durable straps and large side pockets.

B. You can take off the rain cover.

C. There are some extra features.

3   On the radio, you hear a man discussing a cartoon film about dinosaurs.

What aspect of the film disappointed him?

A. the design of the backgrounds

B. the quality of the sonic effects

C. the size of the dinosaurs

4   You overhear a couple talking about keeping fit.

What do they agree about?

A. the need to be more active

B. the high expenses of gym memberships

C. the dangers of too much exercise

5   In a radio play, you hear a woman talking on the phone to a friend.

Where does the woman want her friend to meet her?

A. on the beach

B. at the bank

C. in a shopping mall

6　You hear a student talking to his friend about a meeting with his tutor.

What was the student's purpose in meeting his tutor?

A. to see if there was a part-time job available

B. to ask for financial assistance

C. to request extra help to complete coursework

7　You hear a man talking about learning how to paint landscapes.

What does he say about it?

A. It proved easier than he had thought.

B. It showed him he had some talent.

C. It unlocked doors for him.

8　You turn on the radio and hear a man talking.

What is he talking about?

A. communicating with friends or relatives

B. solving problems

C. helping others

▶ 填空练习

Question 1

I think we really have to _____ _____ _____ __ _____ _____ ___ women's football, to show them it's a great sport, and _____ _____ _____ to play on the _____ _____, things like the Women's World Cup, things like the Olympic Games. That's what _____ _____ _____ to do things. They get to see _____ _____ and they get to see _____ for them to _____, you know, in front of _____ _____. So, I think if we want this sport to _____, this is the message we have to _____ _____.

Question 2

This model from Vango's _____ _____ is one of those bags that you can use _____ _____ on _____ _____ _____. It has _____, _____ _____, large _____ _____ and, as on their bigger bags, there is a _____ ____ _____—very _____ ___ _____ _____ _____. _____, they've _____ __ _____ _____ for a _____ _____ and _____ _____ _____, both of _____ _____ __ _____ _____ _____ _____ ___ other models _____.

Question 3

Well, it's an amazing film. They got all the _____ right, well, almost. They _____ give you a good _____ ___ just _____ _____ _____ _____ were—they make you feel _____ _____…
and the way they move is so _____. Having said that, I feel there _____ _____ _____ _____ _____ ___ ____ _____ _____ : you need to know what their _____ ____ _____,
the kinds of plants these _____ _____ _____…What they had was some _____ ___ _____ _____…But, when it came to the _____ that ____ _____ would have made, you were left in ____ _____—a lot of _____ ___ _____ ____ _____ them _____ _____…

Question 4

Woman: We _____ ___ _____ _____ _____, you know.

Man: Well, there's _____ something in that, but I _____ _____ ____ ____ by the media that I'm not _____ _____.

Woman: Well, doctors want people to _____ ___ _____ ___ _____ too.

Man: So people join a gym, _____ a _____ ____ _____ videos, then within a few weeks _____ ____ ___ ____ it, so it's money____ ___ _____.

Woman: Some people _____ ___ ____ ___ ____.

Man: Yes, and then they _____ _____ it, so that it ____ _____ ___.

Woman: I don't think there's _____ _____ ___ _____ ___ _____ _____.

Question 5

Hi, glad I _____ ___ ____. I'm _____ _____ _____ _____, and guess where I am now?…
Yeah, can you _____ _____ _____? Tell you what, we can both ____ ___ _____ _____ this evening if you like; it won't take long. How about _____ ___ ___ me ____ ___ _____ ____ _____ first?…No, I've got _____ _____—I went past the bank this morning. But if you need some, get it on your way here. OK, so is that _____ then? See you soon. I _____ ____ _____ _____ it!

Question 6

Woman: How did it go then?

Man: Well, I didn't say what I _____ _____. First we talked about the _____ ___ _____ _____ and how much _____ _____ ____ _____ and so on. I mean last month I had to ask for an _____ ____ _____ _____.

Woman: Mmm. I did too. You're _____ _____ there. And?

Man: I finally got to the _____ _____ I'd lost my _____ ____ and had money problems. She _____ that _____ ___ _____ _____ ____ _____ _____ _____ _____ the costs. So I got ____ _____ ___ to _____ ___ and if they accept that, it'll cover the fees for the next six months, so problem solved.

Woman: Great.

Question 7

The best way to learn how to paint is out in the open, with a teacher _____ ____ _____. _____ ____ ___ _____ and painting, you forget about everything else. I thought it _____ ___ _____, and it was, although I wasn't trying to _____ ____ _____. Choosing and _____ the colours, trying to create _____ _____...I was amazed when people _____ ___ and _____ ____ my _____ and said, 'I wish I could do that!' Seeing artists at work had always _____ me, but at school a teacher's report had said: 'Peter has no feeling for art or design.' Then at last, I knew she'd been wrong.

Question 8

It's sometimes hard to _____ _____ ___ _____ _____ on your own. _____ ____ _____ of someone else can _____ ___ _____ _____, and we should _____ that getting the _____ ___ a friend or _____ is __ _____, and not a _____. So often we are ____ ___ believe that _____ ____ _____ is a _____ ___ _____. This simply isn't true. The most _____ _____ are _____ who know how and when to ____ _____ _____, so don't _____ ___ _____ things on your own, if you don't need to. Here are ____ _____ _____ on how to...

▶ 听力原文

Question 1

I think we really have to encourage young girls to get involved in women's football, to show them it's a great sport, and there are opportunities to play on the world stage, things like the Women's World Cup, things like the Olympic Games. That's what inspires young kids to do things. They get to see role models and they get to see opportunities for them to perform, you know, in front of huge audiences. So, I think if we want this sport to develop, this is the message we have to get across.

Question 2

This model from Vango's impressive range is one of those bags that you can use quite happily on long walking trips. It has well-made, comfortable straps, large side pockets and, as on their bigger bags, there is a removable rain cover—very useful in this changeable climate. Interestingly, they've added an internal pocket for a water flask and a key clip, both of which make this bag excellent value compared to other models available.

Question 3

Well, it's an amazing film. They got all the details right, well, almost. They certainly give you a good idea of just how enormous these creatures were—they make you feel really tiny…and the way they move is so believable. Having said that, I feel there should have been more research into the scenic effects: you need to know what their environment was like, the kinds of plants these giants were eating…What they had was some kind of strange landscape…But, when it came to the noises that these beasts would have made, you were left in no doubt—a lot of effort had gone into making them terrifyingly realistic…

Question 4

Woman: We ought to take more exercise, you know.

Man: Well, there's probably something in that, but I resent constantly being told by the media that I'm not active enough.

Woman: Well, doctors want people to take that message on board too.

Man: So people join a gym, spend a fortune on fitness videos, then within a few weeks get fed up with it, so it's money down the drain.

Woman: Some people manage to keep it up.

Man: Yes, and then they start overdoing it, so that it rules their life.

Woman: I don't think there's much danger of that in your case.

Question 5

Hi, glad I caught you in. I'm phoning from my mobile, and guess where I am now?…Yeah, can you hear the waves? Tell you what, we can both do the shopping together this evening if you like; it won't take long. How about coming to join me for a couple of hours first?…No, I've got enough cash—I went past the bank this morning. But if you need some, get it on your way here. OK, so is that settled then? See you soon. I promise you won't regret it!

Question 6

Woman: How did it go then?

Man: Well, I didn't say what I wanted immediately. First we talked about the difficulty of the course and how much pressure it puts on students and so on. I mean last month I had to ask for an extension on both my assignments.

Woman: Mmm. I did too. You're not alone there. And?

Man: I finally got to the point saying I'd lost my part-time job and had money problems. She mentioned that there were special grants for those having difficulty with the costs. So I got an application form to fill in and if they accept that, it'll cover the fees for the next six months, so problem solved.

Woman: Great.

Question 7

The best way to learn how to paint is out in the open, with a teacher giving you guidance. Sitting on a stool and painting, you forget about everything else. I thought it would be demanding, and it was, although I wasn't trying to become a professional. Choosing and mixing the colours, trying to create perfect clouds…I was amazed when people passed by and peered over my shoulder and said, 'I wish I could do that!' Seeing artists at work had always fascinated me, but at school a teacher's report had said: 'Peter has no feeling for art or design.' Then at last, I knew she'd been wrong.

Question 8

It's sometimes hard to deal with a difficult situation on your own. Having the support of someone else can make all the difference, and we should recognise that getting the aid of a friend or relative is a strength, and not a weakness. So often we are led to believe that sharing our challenges is a sign of failure. This simply isn't true. The most successful people are those who know how and when to ask for help, so don't battle on with things on your own, if you don't need to. Here are a few tips on how to…

FCE LISTENING

FCE LISTENING

FCE LISTENING

FCE LISTENING

FCE LISTENING

FCE LISTENING

FCE LISTENING

FCE LISTENING

FCE LISTENING

SECTION 1

▶ 听力原题

Part 2

You will hear an interview with Elizabeth Holmes about her experience working in Africa. For Questions 9–18, complete the sentences.

Volunteering in Africa

Elizabeth worked for a | **9** | before she went to Africa.

Elizabeth first found out about working as a volunteer from a | **10** | she saw at the dentist's.

The course in London that Elizabeth attended was called | **11** |.

Elizabeth's job in Africa was to teach | **12** | how to market their goods.

On arrival in Africa, Elizabeth spent | **13** | doing a training course with other volunteers.

Elizabeth used a | **14** | to travel short distances in Africa.

Elizabeth feels that she got on best with | **15** | in the area of Africa where she lived.

Back in England, Elizabeth found that she was disturbed by the | **16** | in the city.

At the moment, Elizabeth buys and sells | **17** | from Africa.

Nowadays, Elizabeth spends more time on her favourite pastime, which is

| **18** |.

▶ 填空练习

Interviewer: Visitors to the small Devon village of Whimple _____ ____ _____ _____ _____ _____ as they pass the garden of Elizabeth Holmes. In the middle of the garden _____ _____ ___ _____ _____ ___, a _____ of the two years Elizabeth spent in Africa as a volunteer. Elizabeth, what _____ ____ to leave your _____ _____ in a _____ _____ and go to Africa?

Elizabeth: Well, I'd _____ _____ _____ _____ _____. I wanted to see the _____ _____, not just _____ _____. Then, I was at the _____ _____ _____, _____ ___ _____ ___, and I'd read _____ _____ _____ in the waiting room, so I _____ _____ _____ ___ _____—it was all about volunteers working in Africa.

Interviewer: And it _____ you?

Elizabeth: Yes, I _____ ____ _____ _____ and _____ and _____. I had an _____ _____ and ____ _____ _____ _____. Then just before I left for Africa, there was a _____ _____ ___ _____, which they call 'Changes' and which _____ ___ _____ ____ ____ what you're letting yourself in for.

Interviewer: What _____ _____ could you _____?

Elizabeth: I had a _____ ___ _____ and I had _____ _____ at one time. What they wanted to ____ ____ _____ Africa to do was to _____ _____ _____ in the _____ _____ ___ _____ _____. I ____ ____ _____ fifteen other _____, all _____ ___ ___ _____ _____, like _____, _____, and so on. When we got there, we _____ _____ ___ _____ a _____ ____ at a training centre _____ _____ _____ _____ _____ and the _____ ___ _____ _____—you know, _____ and _____ _____ _____. _____, there was a _____ and it only _____ ___ _____ __ ____ _____—not enough really.

Interviewer: Did it take a long time to _____ _____ ____ _____ _____ _____?

Elizabeth: I found it _____ _____ ____ the first few weeks, but after that I _____ ___ _____ _____. My area covered 1,200 square kilometres, and I had a _____ ____ _____ _____, but for _____ ____ _____ I ____ a _____.

Interviewer: How did you _____ _____ _____ _____ _____ _____ _____?

Elizabeth: Very well. The men were _____ _____, but they _____ ___ _____ _____ _____ — _____ the women, who were _____ _____ _____ ___ _____. They _____ ___ ____ ____ ____ and ____ _____ ___ _____ _____ ___ _____ and their children. I _____ ___ _____ _____ _____ from England and we'd _____ _____ _____ ___ _____.

Interviewer: I _____ ____ _____ it very _____ when you _____ to England?

Elizabeth: Yes, I _____ did. After two years of _____ _____ _____, I found the _____ _____ _____ —just the _____ _____ ___ _____. Also, the _____ _____ me. I had to _____ _____ _____ _____ in the city to a _____ _____ in the country just to _____ _____ ___ _____ _____ and quiet I'd _____ _____ ___ in Africa.

Interviewer: And what are you _____ ___ _____ _____?

Elizabeth: Well, I didn't want to just go back to _____ ___ _____ else's office, so I ____ ____ _____ _____ _____, which I run from home. I _____ ___ African _____. I _____ some _____ _____ _____ ___ me as _____ and everyone _____ _____ in Britain. However, I'm still ____ _____ _____ the _____ that _____ me to Africa ___ ___ _____. I organise _____ ___ _____ _____ and ____ _____ about my _____ ___ _____ _____ _____ ___ ___.

Interviewer: ___ the _____ ___ _____ _____ you ___ ___?

Elizabeth: Oh yes, in many ways. I used to _____ all my time _____, but now I _____ _____ I _____ _____ _____ _____ _____ —my favourite hobby.

Interviewer: Well, I'd like to thank Elizabeth for coming into the studio today. If you're interested in…

▶ 听力原文

Interviewer: Visitors to the small Devon village of Whimple might be forgiven for looking twice as they pass the garden of Elizabeth Holmes. In the middle of the garden there stands a traditional African hut, a reminder of the two years Elizabeth spent in Africa as a volunteer. Elizabeth, what persuaded you to leave your secure job in a travel agent's and go to Africa?

Elizabeth: Well, I'd been feeling restless for ages. I wanted to see the real world, not just tourist places. Then, I was at the dentist's one day, waiting to go in, and I'd read all the magazines in the waiting room, so I started looking at a poster—it was all about volunteers working in Africa.

Interviewer: And it interested you?

Elizabeth: Yes, I took down the name and address and applied. I had an interview locally and did some aptitude tests. Then just before I left for Africa, there was a training weekend in London, which they call 'Changes' and which gives you some idea of what you're letting yourself in for.

Interviewer: What particular skills could you offer?

Elizabeth: I had a degree in economics and I had done some teaching at one time. What they wanted to send me to Africa to do was to train local farmers in the marketing of their produce. I flew out with fifteen other volunteers, all going to do different things, like nursing, teaching, and so on. When we got there, we were supposed to have a four-week course at a training centre learning something about the local culture and the basics of the language—you know, greetings and things like that. Anyway, there was a problem and it only lasted three weeks in the end—not enough really.

Interviewer: Did it take a long time to get used to your new lifestyle?

Elizabeth: I found it quite difficult for the first few weeks, but after that I settled in very well. My area covered 1,200 square kilometres, and I had a truck for long-distance travel, but for more local trips I rode a motorbike.

Interviewer: How did you get on with the local people?

Elizabeth: Very well. The men were very polite, but they tended to keep their distance—unlike the women, who were always inviting me to meals. They showed me how they wove and dyed material to make clothes for themselves and their children. I used to get magazines sent from England and we'd spend ages looking at them.

Interviewer: I expect you found it very different when you returned to England?

Elizabeth: Yes, I certainly did. After two years of living very simply, I found the supermarkets especially overwhelming—just the enormous choice of food. Also, the traffic disturbed me. I had to move from my flat in the city to a small cottage in the country just to get some of the peace and quiet I'd become accustomed to in Africa.

Interviewer: And what are you working on at the moment?

Elizabeth: Well, I didn't want to just go back to working in someone else's office, so I set up my own business, which I run from home. I deal in African furniture. I brought some small pieces back with me as souvenirs and everyone loved them in Britain. However, I'm still in touch with the organisation that sent me to Africa as a volunteer. I organise events to raise funds and give talks about my experience to encourage other people to go.

Interviewer: Has the experience in Africa changed you at all?

Elizabeth: Oh yes, in many ways. I used to spend all my time working, but now I make sure I have more time for gardening—my favourite hobby.

Interviewer: Well, I'd like to thank Elizabeth for coming into the studio today. If you're interested in…

SECTION 2

▶ 听力原题

Part 2

You will hear an announcement about an evening's programmes on Radio Pearl. For Questions 9–18, complete the sentences.

7.30 pm 'Art Review': Student Art Exhibition

This evening's programme is taking place at the [**9**] in London.

The exhibition is of work by students in the [**10**] year of their art course.

At the exhibition, you can see things as different as curtains and [**11**].

Some of the works of art have been made using [**12**] technology.

8.00 pm Play: 'The Vanishing Lady'

In the play, a young couple on train think they hear the sound of someone using a

[**13**].

A [**14**] tells the couple about an old lady whom he has seen.

After writing this play, the author, Porten, became a writer for [**15**].

9.30 pm 'Business Scenes': Interview with Peter Field

Peter used to work for a [**16**].

Peter says the material he uses for his boats is a particular kind of [**17**].

Peter collects [**18**] as a hobby.

▶ 填空练习

And now a look at some of this evening's programmes on Radio Pearl. At 7.30 we have Art Review, a programme which ____ _____ _____ ___ _____ _____ our _____, with its mix of _____ _____ ___ _____ _____, and _____ _____ ___ ___ _____ who _____ ____ _____ ___ _____. Today we'll be going to London to the National Museum, which ____ _____ _____ _____ ___ _____, and this _____ ___ is always _____ because it _____ _____ by _____ _____.

This year is _____ _____ ___ everything is the work of _____ art students from a _____ _____. You'll be _____ ___ _____ _____ ___ _____ you can see. _____ _____ _____ _____ to glass work, and I _____ there are ___ _____ ____ _____ 2,000 works ____ _____. There is an _____ ___ ____ _____ _____, and of course _____ _____ _____ how _____ _____ ___ __ _____ in art. If you want to buy _____ ___ _____ _____, it will _____ ____ _____ from £25 up to £2,000. So for more information on what can be seen, where and for how much, tune in to Radio Pearl tonight at 7.30.

Then at 8.00, there's another in our _____ _____ _____ _____, and tonight it's *The Vanishing Lady*, _____ Margaret Louden.

_____, two young people _____ _____ ___ ___ ___ _____ when they are walking through a _____ ___ ___ _____ and _____ ____ ___ _____ that sounds to them like a gun _____ _____. They _____ ___ the next _____ which is _____ _____ with its doors _____ _____ and _____. Then in the restaurant car they ask the first person they meet—who _____ ___ __ ___ _____—if he also _____ ____ _____.

'No', he says, and _____ ___ ___ _____ them that an old lady is in the carriage—he just saw her going back in there. But when they _____, of course, she's gone. Some say the lady _____ _____, but others _____ _____ they saw her. Who's _____ ___ _____, or is _____ ___ ____ _____ _____? Find out at 8 o'clock tonight. It's a brilliant play by Porten, and also his last before he moved on to writing for films.

Finally, for those of you who like sailing. Business Scenes at 9.30 p.m. _____ ____ the _____ ____ and a _____ ___ _____ ___ _____, Canadian businessman Peter Field. In 1995, Peter was a _____ ___ __ _____ _____, but he left that job to go on a _____ _____. He had wanted a _____ ____, but _____ ___ _____ in the ___ _____, building boats. His new company has many _____ _____ _____ boats _____ from $1–2 million, which Peter _____ _____ _____ ___ ____ _____ even if they _____ _____ _____ ___ _____ _____…It's all in the type of metal you use, as he explains tonight.

And we also hear about Peter's _____ _____. You would think that a man in his line of work _____ _____ _____ _____ and ships, _____ _____ the old maps which are his _____ _____! If you tune in this evening, you'll find out how he started his collection and _____ ___ _____ ____ _____ ___ _____ to it!

Well, back to this afternoon's programmes…

▶ 听力原文

And now a look at some of this evening's programmes on Radio Pearl. At 7.30 we have Art Review, a programme which has fast become a favourite among our listeners, with its mix of in-depth reports on artistic events, and revealing interviews with the artists who regularly come into the studio. Today we'll be going to London to the National Museum, which holds approximately five events a year, and this particular one is always popular because it features work by student artists.

This year is no exception as everything is the work of final-year art students from a local college. You'll be surprised at the variety of things you can see. Exhibits range from curtains to glass work, and I understand there are a total of nearly 2,000 works on display. There is an excellent use of raw materials, and of course many exhibits demonstrate how industrial technology can be employed in art. If you want to buy any of the exhibits, it will cost you anything from £25 up to £2,000. So for more information on what can be seen, where and for how much, tune in to Radio Pearl tonight at 7.30.

Then at 8.00, there's another in our series of classic plays, and tonight it's *The Vanishing Lady*, starring Margaret Louden.

Briefly, two young people become caught up in a thrilling adventure when they are walking through a carriage on a train and suddenly hear a noise that sounds to them like a gun being fired. They rush into the next carriage which is completely empty with its doors swinging backwards and forwards.

Then in the restaurant car they ask the first person they meet—who happens to be a waiter—if he also heard the sound.

'No', he says, and goes on to tell them that an old lady is in the carriage—he just saw her going back in there. But when they return, of course, she's gone. Some say the lady never existed, but others are sure they saw her. Who's telling the truth, or is everyone on the train lying? Find out at 8 o'clock tonight. It's a brilliant play by Porten, and also his last before he moved on to writing for films.

Finally, for those of you who like sailing. Business Scenes at 9.30 p.m. brings you the 'unsinkable' boat and a chance to meet its maker, Canadian businessman Peter Field. In 1995, Peter was a manager in a computer company, but he left that job to go on a world cruise. He had wanted a stress-free life, but ended up back in the rat race, building boats. His new company has many products including luxury boats costing from $1–2 million, which Peter claims will suffer no serious damage even if they hit an iceberg at full speed...It's all in the type of metal you use, as he explains tonight.

And we also hear about Peter's unusual collection. You would think that a man in his line of work would collect model boats and ships, rather than the old maps which are his real passion! If you tune in this evening, you'll find out how he started his collection and how he hunts for items to add to it!

Well, back to this afternoon's programmes...

SECTION 3

▶ 听力原题

Part 2

You will hear a man called Peter Welby, who makes small models of buildings, talking about his work. For Questions 9–18, complete the sentences.

The Model Maker

Before becoming a model maker, Peter did a course in ☐ **9** at a college.

Peter compares his job to the type of work done by a ☐ **10**.

In Peter's hardest job, he was given some ☐ **11** of the building to work from.

Peter's most enjoyable job was making a model of a ☐ **12** for an exhibition.

Most of Peter's work is exported to ☐ and **13**.

Peter says his models look best when they have ☐ **14** directed onto them.

Peter's model of Marney House measures ☐ **15** in height.

The Marney House model took a long time to make because it had so many ☐ **16** and roof tiles.

The roof tiles on the model of Marney House are made of ☐ **17**.

Peter uses watercolour paint to reproduce the effects of the weather and ☐ **18**.

▶ 填空练习

My job is _____. I make small _____ ___ _____ _____ and other _____. It might seem _____ _____ _____, but I knew when I was at school that it was what I _____ ___ _____. So I did a _____ _____, not in art or _____ as you _____ _____, but in _____. Because of the _____ ___ _____ _____ ___ _____, it was _____ ___ __ _____. Although later, of course, I had to _____ ___ _____ to other _____ ___ _____. When I make a _____ ____ ___ ___ _____, often _____ _____ ___ _____ ___ _____ ___ _____ or even _____ _____ over the years, so I have to work _____ ___ ____ _____ ___ _____ _____ _____ like. _____, I think there's _____ ___ ____ ___ _____ ___ _____ what I do and what a _____ does… _____ _____ _____, _____ ___ ____ _____ …

I've _____ _____ ___ _____ _____ now. The _____ _____ I've ever had was from Ireland. I was _____ ___ ___ ___ _____ ___ _____ ___ a large house which had _____ _____ years before. They just gave me a few old photos to use, as there was ____ _____ _____ ___ _____. I've done _____ _____ ___ _____ _____, everything from _____ _____ to the _____ _____ _____. The one I liked most, though, was where I had to _____ ___ _____. The original building was gone, but this time there were _____ _____to work from. My _____ _____ _____ _____ ___ ___ _____ called 'All the World's a Stage' here in London. It was fun because I could go and look at it every day if I wanted to; see how people _____ _____ to it. _____, though, I don't see my models again after I've _____ them, as 80% of them are _____ ____ to Japan or Canada, _____ _____ _____ _____ _____ _____ _____ ___ . I _____ ____ ___ _____ _____, however, about how the _____ _____ ___ _____. The _____ ____ _____ they should stand, _____ _____ ___ _____ _____ _____ should be, and also about lighting, because the colours and _____ _____ ____ _____ _____ if there's _____ _____ _____ _____ them. _____ ____ _____.

And that's _____ _____ ___ _____ _____ _____ _____, a model of a very interesting old building called Marney House. The _____ _____ ___ _____ ___ ___ _____ and wanted a model to _____ ____ _____. The detail work was very _____ _____, as I had to _____ ___ _____ ___ ___ model just one hundred and forty centimetres high, which is

39

seventy-six _____ _____ _____ _____ _____ _____...that's small, yet everything has

to be there. It _____ _____ _____ ____ _____ _____ I've ever done before, _____

_____ I had to do all of the 150 windows...____ _____ _____ ____ _____! There were

times, ____ ____ _____, when I found myself _____ ___ _____ _____ I'd ever _____

____ _____ on in the first place. On top of that, I had to make every _____ ____ ____ ____

_____ ___ _____ ___ _____ out of paper. Mind you, when I had _____ ____

_____, I knew the _____ _____ was over, and that the rest would be quite fun. Doing things

like the _____ _____ _____ _____ _____ _____, because every one's different...and I

_____ _____ _____ _____ _____ _____ _____ _____ to get the _____ _____

of the _____ _____ _____. When I'd finished all that, the only _____ _____

_____ that, of course, the _____ _____ _____ like a _____ ____ a new building. So I did what

I usually do, which is to _____ _____ the outside of the model with watercolour, so that it looks

as if, over the years, it's been _____ ____ _____ and rain, and also _____, of course. The

_____ were very _____ _____ ____ _____, and I'm glad I can go and see it from time to

time. _____ is a great job, and I'd _____ ___ ____ anyone with _____ and an eye _____

_____.

▶ 听力原文

My job is model-making. I make small copies of large buildings and other structures. It might seem a

strange job, but I knew when I was at school that it was what I wanted to do. So I did a college course,

not in art or architecture as you might expect, but in woodwork. Because of the concentration on fine

detail it requires, it was ideal for a model-maker. Although later, of course, I had to adapt my skills to

other materials as well. When I make a model of an old building, often original parts of the building

have been damaged or even completely demolished over the years, so I have to work hard to find out

what they must have been like. Actually, I think there's quite a lot in common between what I do and

what a detective does...tracking down clues, working things out...

I've done quite a few jobs now. The toughest commission I've ever had was from Ireland. I was asked

to do a model of part of a large house which had burnt down years before. They just gave me a few old

photos to use, as there was no actual building to copy. I've done all sorts of buildings since, everything

from grand castles to the most ordinary farmhouse. The one I liked most, though, was where I had to

rebuild a theatre. The original building was gone, but this time there were detailed drawings to work from. My model was then shown in an exhibition called 'All the World's a Stage' here in London. It was fun because I could go and look at it every day if I wanted to; see how people were reacting to it. Generally, though, I don't see my models again after I've delivered them, as 80% of them are shipped out to Japan or Canada, with the rest shared between England and France. I do try to give pretty careful instructions, however, about how the models should be displayed. The height at which they should stand, how large the space around them should be, and also about lighting, because the colours and details come out most clearly if there's electric light directly above them. Daylight's too pale.

And that's particularly true of my most recent project, a model of a very interesting old building called Marney House. The owners decided to open it to the public and wanted a model to display for visitors. The detail work was very challenging indeed, as I had to reduce the original to a model just one hundred and forty centimetres high, which is seventy-six times smaller than the real building...that's small, yet everything has to be there. It actually took longer than any model I've ever done before, mainly because I had to do all of the 150 windows...a real test of patience! There were times, to be honest, when I found myself regretting the fact that I'd ever taken the project on in the first place. On top of that, I had to make every single one of the thousands of roof tiles individually out of paper. Mind you, when I had finished that process, I knew the hardest part was over, and that the rest would be quite fun. Doing things like the statues along the front was enjoyable, because every one's different...and I spent some happy hours playing around with colours to get the exact reproduction of the original interior walls. When I'd finished all that, the only remaining problem was that, of course, the whole thing looked like a model of a new building. So I did what I usually do, which is to carefully wash the outside of the model with watercolour, so that it looks as if, over the years, it's been affected by wind and rain, and also pollution, of course. The owners were very pleased with the result, and I'm glad I can go and see it from time to time. Model-making is a great job, and I'd recommend it to anyone with patience and an eye for detail.

SECTION 4

▶ 听力原题

Part 2

You will hear an interview with a man called Richard Porter who is a maker of musical instruments called organs. For Questions 9–18, complete the sentences.

Musical Instrument Maker

Richard's first ambition was to be a [_____ **9**].

Richard makes organs which are used in [_____ **10**] and churches worldwide.

It costs [_____ **11**] pounds to buy one of the organs which Richard makes.

According to Richard, personal [_____ **12**] provide him with most of his overseas clients.

Richards says that he is involved in [_____ **13**] organs, as well as building and selling them.

In terms of raw materials, only the [_____ **14**] that Richard uses comes from Britain.

Richard's new workshop will be in a building that was once used as a [_____ **15**].

Richard will have to work in a [_____ **16**] as well as in his new workshop.

The only thing that Richard will have to pay for in his new workshop is the [_____ **17**].

The new workshop will be perfect for the instruments Richard makes because it is a [_____ **18**] place.

▶ 填空练习

Interviewer: Good evening and welcome to the programme where, as you know, we _____ _____ and _____ _____ _____ who _____ _____ _____ _____. Today, we're talking to Richard Porter, who makes large concert _____ __ __ _____. Richard, tell us, just how did you _____ _____ _____ _____ __ _____?

Richard: Well, I play the piano and, as a child, I had a good teacher who wrote her own music, and I always wanted to be a composer too. However, my parents _____ ___ _____ _____ ___ _____ __ ____ was go to college and study how to _____ _____ _____, rather than play them, because they saw _____ __ __ _____ in that. And now, I make the organs which are _____ ___ _____ and _____ _____ all around the world. The one thing that I never _____ __ ___ ___ _____ __ _____, which is what I am now really, as well as _____ ___ _____ _____.

Interviewer: So, when did you _____ _____ _____?

Richard: About five years ago. I started from a room in my house, but now I have my _____ _____.

Interviewer: So, it must pay.

Richard: Well, an organ sells at £9,500, which means _____ _____ _____for me I suppose.

Interviewer: And _____ _____ _____ ___ _____ ___ _____ one?

Richard: It might take me three months ____ _____ ____, and when I say three months, I mean three months of _____ _____ _____ a week. Although that _____ __ ____, I have to say I don't _____ because I love the work and I get to _____ _____ _____ _____ _____. Most of my _____ are from _____ _____ and they're nearly all the _____ __ _____ _____. I _____ __ _____ these days.

Interviewer: So, you _____ __ _____ _____ ___ it?

Richard: Not really. The _____ _____ ___ of my business is _____ _____ _____, _____ ____ _____ ones, so they can be used for concerts and _____ _____. That can _____ ___ ___ ___ £300 each time. Which is just as well, because I do _____ __ ____ _____ _____ to buy the ____ _____ for the larger organs. There's a lot of _____ ___ _____ before I can start to build. I get the _____ _____ Britain, but _____ ___ ___ _____ _____ come from France or Germany.

Interviewer: And I _____ you've _____ ___ ____ _____ recently?

Richard: Yes. I've decided to _____ ____ _____ ___ _____ my workshop to a _____ _____ that has _____ _____ in Lincolnshire, about a hundred miles away.

Interviewer: So, you're moving house as well?

Richard: Yes. We're _____ _____ ___ _____ _____ time.

Interviewer: Tell me about the new _____.

Richard: It is a _____ ____ _____ _____ ___ the Town Hall in a small market town. ____ _____ ___ _____ the workshop, I've _____ ___ _____ forty days a year _____ ___ ___ _____ _____. There is a small museum in the town that has _____ _____, but is only open on _____ _____ in the year.

Interviewer: And is that something you're _____ _____ ___?

Richard: Not really, but it _____ _____ I save around £4,000 a year because _____ _____ _____ ___ _____ ___ the workshop is _____ _____. That's the _____ _____ _____ the place. It's also very _____ ___ _____ new house, so I'll have the _____ ___ _____ ___ _____ each morning, which is nice.

Interviewer: Is it easy to _____ ___ _____ that is _____ ___ ___ _____?

Richard: No, it isn't. It's very _____ ___ _____ ____ _____ ___ ____ _____ so the _____ ___ ___ ____. _____ ___ ___ _____ I've worked in so far have been dry enough. The new workshop is _____ ___ _____ _____.

Interviewer: Oh right. Well, _____ ___ _____ ___ _____ in that new _____. Now, I think you're going to play us a _____ ___ ___ _____ _____ ___ _____ yourself...

▶ 听力原文

Interviewer: Good evening and welcome to the programme where, as you know, we go out and talk to people who run their own companies. Today, we're talking to Richard Porter, who makes large concert organs as a profession. Richard, tell us, just how did you get into this area of work?

Richard: Well, I play the piano and, as a child, I had a good teacher who wrote her own music, and I always wanted to be a composer too. However, my parents persuaded me that what I needed to do was go to college and study how to make musical instruments, rather than play them, because they saw more of a future in that. And now, I make the organs which are played in churches and concert halls all around the world. The one thing that I never intended to do was become a businessman, which is what I am now really, as well as being an instrument maker.

Interviewer: So, when did you start making organs?

Richard: About five years ago. I started from a room in my house, but now I have my own workshop.

Interviewer: So, it must pay.

Richard: Well, an organ sells at £9,500, which means around £3,500 profit for me I suppose.

Interviewer: And how long does it take to build one?

Richard: It might take me three months to complete one, and when I say three months, I mean three months of working seventy hours a week. Although that sounds a lot, I have to say I don't mind because I love the work and I get to meet lots of interesting people. Most of my commissions are from overseas clients and they're nearly all the result of personal contacts. I rarely use advertising these days.

Interviewer: So, you make a living out of it?

Richard: Not really. The most profitable part of my business is actually mending organs, generally old large ones, so they can be used for concerts and recording sessions. That can earn me up to £300 each time. Which is just as well, because I do need to have money available to buy the raw materials for the larger organs. There's a lot of investment to make before I can start to build. I get the wood from Britain, but most of the other components come from France or Germany.

Interviewer: And I understand you've made a big decision recently?

Richard: Yes. I've decided to take the opportunity to move my workshop to a former schoolroom that has become available in Lincolnshire, about a hundred miles away.

Interviewer: So, you're moving house as well?

Richard: Yes. We're moving there in three months' time.

Interviewer: Tell me about the new workshop.

Richard: It is a lovely old building attached to the Town Hall in a small market town. In return for using the workshop, I've agreed to spend forty days a year working as a museum attendant. There is a small museum in the town that has visiting exhibitions, but is only open on certain days in the year.

Interviewer: And is that something you're looking forward to?

Richard: Not really, but it means that I save around £4,000 a year because apart from paying the heating bill the workshop is rent free. That's the great thing about the place. It's also very close to our new house, so I'll have the luxury of walking to work each morning, which is nice.

Interviewer: Is it easy to find a building that is suitable as a workshop?

Richard: No, it isn't. It's very easy for the instruments to get damaged so the environment must be dry. None of the buildings I've worked in so far have been dry enough. The new workshop is perfect in that respect.

Interviewer: Oh right. Well, best of luck to you in that new project. Now, I think you're going to play us a piece on an organ which you built yourself...

CHAPTER 3 FCE LISTENING PART 3

FCE LISTENING

FCE LISTENING

FCE LISTENING

FCE LISTENING

FCE LISTENING

FCE LISTENING

FCE LISTENING

FCE LISTENING

FCE LISTENING

SECTION 1

▶ 听力原题

Part 3

You will hear five different employees talking about what makes a good boss. For Questions 19–23, choose which of the opinions (A–F) each speaker expresses. Use the letters only once. There is one extra letter which you do not need to use.

A good boss should

A. allow staff to take decisions.

B. encourage staff to work in teams.

C. listen to complaints from staff.

D. give information on individual progress.

E. have good qualifications.

F. set an example of hard work.

Speaker 1	19
Speaker 2	20
Speaker 3	21
Speaker 4	22
Speaker 5	23

▶ 填空练习

Speaker 1

Man: Some people still think that _____ ____ _____, not made. They say, __ _____ ____ _____ you study and how many _____ you _____, at the end of the day, if you've got _____ _____, such as __ _____ _____, that's all _____ _____. I think _____ _____. _____ is all about _____ _____. If a boss says to me, for example, 'Look, your computer skills _____ _____', I'll think, 'Right, this person ____ __ _____ in computing, I don't, so he must be right.' But if it's the other way round, then you feel, well, maybe I should be boss!

Speaker 2

Woman: Well, _____ _____ ___ leaders that I actually _____…are not the…____ _____ __ _____…with a degree ___ _____ and a _____ that nobody can do things __ _____ __ ____ ___. One thing I've learned from all my _____ __ _____ ____ is that, to be a really good boss, you have to __ _____ __ _____ the people under you to _____ __ _____ _____…_____ a situation in which other people can _____. Of course this does not mean the boss's job is any easier; it's still a _____, but __ _____ _____ _____ for everyone.

Speaker 3

Woman: Since I left school, I've _____ __ _____ ____ _____ _____ _____, and I must say I'm _____ ____ _____ ___ _____ it is to ____ ____ ____ ____ ____ _____ _____ your work. To _____ all my _____, I need to be told when I'm doing something well, and also the areas where I _____ _____…I think _____ _____ you ___ _____ and _____ _____, the better. _____ you _____ ___ _____…Some of my _____ don't _____ _____ ___; when I say it's good to _____ _____ ____ _____ boss, they think I'm _____ ___ ____ better than them.

Speaker 4

Man: Of course we all want bosses who are _____ and who _____ _____ to the job, and I must say, ____ ____ _____, most people who _____ ____ _____ _____ __ _____ _____ _____. However, what really _____ is the _____ ____ _____ _____ together. _____ often _____ _____ people to work ____ _____ _____, kind of, _____ _____, because they are _____ ____ ____ _____ ____ _____, they think maybe they'll _____, or even _____ _____ _____ the leader…Such leaders need to ____ ____ _____ _____, to _____ ____ _____ _____ ___ _____…

Speaker 5

Man: Well, in the organisation where I work, each _____ ____ ___ _____, a boss… and because I've _____ ___ ____ of _____ _____, I've had six different bosses! I must say there's been _____ _____ _____ _____ _____…_____ that we are _____ _____ to do an _____ _____ ____ _____ work and some of the bosses don't _____ _____ ____ _____ _____ hours, like _____ ____ ____ us. It is _____ ____ after work, they may _____ __ _____ _____ _____ _____, or meet _____ _____ ____ _____ to _____ _____, but this only _____ _____…

▶ 听力原文

Speaker 1

Man: Some people still think that leaders are born, not made. They say, no matter how hard you study and how many diplomas you collect, at the end of the day, if you've got natural skills, such as a strong character, that's all you'll need. I think that's nonsense. Leadership is all about commanding respect. If a boss says to me, for example, 'Look, your computer skills need upgrading', I'll think, 'Right, this person has a degree in computing, I don't, so he must be right.' But if it's the other way round, then you feel, well, maybe I should be boss!

Speaker 2

Woman: Well, the sort of leaders that I actually admire…are not the…top dogs in suits…with a degree in management and a belief that nobody can do things as well as they can. One thing I've learned from all my experience in different jobs is that, to be a really good boss, you have to be good at encouraging the people under you to decide on important issues… creating a situation in which other people can shine. Of course this does not mean the boss's job is any easier; it's still a challenge, but so much more rewarding for everyone.

Speaker 3

Woman: Since I left school, I've done a number of short-term office jobs, and I must say I'm beginning to realise how important it is to have the right sort of person directing your work. To develop all my potential, I need to be told when I'm doing something well, and also the areas where I could improve…I think the earlier you get formal and informal feedback, the better. Otherwise you develop bad habits…Some of my workmates don't agree with me; when I say it's good to meet regularly with your boss, they think I'm trying to be better than them.

Speaker 4

Man: Of course we all want bosses who are knowledgeable and who bring energy to the job, and I must say, in my opinion, most people who reach top job positions do possess these qualities. However, what really matters is the ability to bring people together. Leaders often mistakenly encourage people to work on their own, kind of, in isolation, because they are afraid of the strengths of groups, they think maybe they'll criticise, or even join forces against the leader… Such leaders need to go on management courses, to look at good examples of leadership…

Speaker 5

Man: Well, in the organisation where I work, each department has a leader, a boss… and because I've worked in six of these departments, I've had six different bosses! I must say there's been very little to complain about…except that we are being asked to do an enormous amount of extra work and some of the bosses don't seem to be doing long hours, like the rest of us. It is true that after work, they may have to attend special management courses, or meet individual members of staff to discuss performance, but this only happens occasionally…

SECTION 2

▶ 听力原题

Part 3

You will hear five different people talking about the way they study. For Questions 19–23, choose from the list (A–F) which of the opinions each speaker expresses. Use the letters only once. There is one extra letter which you do not need to use.

A. Music helps me concentrate when I'm studying.

B. I study best in the morning when I can think clearly.

C. I realise I study better when I'm outside in the open air.

D. I find I can concentrate better when I study with a friend.

E. It is much easier for me to study late at night.

F. I prefer to study when I'm lying down.

Speaker 1	19
Speaker 2	20
Speaker 3	21
Speaker 4	22
Speaker 5	23

▶ 填空练习

Speaker 1

Girl: I must say, I've _____ _____ ___ _____ to study at home. I've tried all ____ ___ _____. One of my friends _____ ___ _____ _____, _____ ____ ___ _____ ___ _____ _____. I try that from time to time and it's nice and _____, though my _____ _____ ___ _____ ___ ____ and I find I'm looking at the trees, or people _____ ___, _____ _____ at my notes. I think better in my bedroom, where it's nice and quiet. I've got a _____ _____ _____ ___ _____ my computer on, and I set my _____ _____ and work with a _____ _____ before everyone else's up.

Speaker 2

Boy: You know _____ _____ I ____ _____? Well, it's _____ but I find people _____ really _____ _____ _____ when I'm trying to study, ____ I _____ ever work with classmate, although it's _____ ____ ____. You'd think that the _____ _____ _____ ___ _____ _____ _____ for me then—an _____ _____ and ____ _____. You always get ___ ____ people _____ and _____ though and that _____ ___. What I _____ ___ _____ now is ____ ___ ___ _____ _____ and have something _____ _____, it doesn't matter what. That _____ ___ _____ else and I _____ _____ the work ___ ___ _____.

Speaker 3

Girl: When I do my homework I have to feel right. After _____ ___ __ _____ chair all day, I need to _____ ____ _____ __ _____ __ __ ___ ____. Mum says I cannot _____ _____ like that, but _____ I don't _____ _____ ___ _____ ___ I don't go on too late, and I have the window open to ___ _____ _____ ___. I'd love to work with music on, a lot of my friends do, and they say it really ___ ___ _____. The point is I like music too much—it takes over from whatever I'm _____ __ __ _____.

Speaker 4

Boy: I'm _____ _____ _____ _____ _____. I make _____ so that I can _____ ___ _____ ____ before the _____, but I don't _____ __ them. I've _____ everything—____ _____, quiet rooms, fresh air. _____ ____ I'm wide _____ and there's nothing to _____ _____, the work still doesn't get done. I was _____ _____ _____ last week, when Mary _____ _____ and asked if she could ____ ___ ____ _____—hers is too _____ and _____. I've never worked with a friend before and so I said 'No', but she was _____. _____, I gave in and it really _____ ___ for us both. I _____ _____ it!

Speaker 5

Girl: I really like some of the _____ I'm doing this year, _____ maths and _____. I don't _____ _____ _____ ____ ____, although some of the homework _____ we're given are quite _____, so I need to be able to work _____. That's often ___ _____ _____ in our house, _____ I put it off _____ everyone's ____ _____. Did you know that my younger brother, Fred, plays the guitar in a band? I love some of their music, it's really cool, you'd love it too, but it's _____ _____ to work _____ ___ _____.

▶ 听力原文

Speaker 1

Girl: I must say, I've never found it easy to study at home. I've tried all sorts of places. One of my friends prefers to study outside, lying on a rug in the garden. I try that from time to time and it's nice and airy, though my concentration tends to wander a bit and I find I'm looking at the trees, or people passing by, rather than at my notes. I think better in my bedroom, where it's nice and quiet. I've got a large desk there to put my computer on, and I set my alarm early and work with a fresh mind before everyone else's up.

Speaker 2

Boy: You know how sociable I am normally? Well, it's strange but I find people talking really puts me off when I'm trying to study, so I hardly ever work with classmate, although it's much more fun. You'd think that the faculty library would be the best place for me then— an academic atmosphere and no distractions. You always get a few people whispering and coughing though and that annoys me. What I frequently do instead now is put on my personal stereo and have something blasting away, it doesn't matter what. That blocks out everything else and I get through the work in no time.

Speaker 3

Girl: When I do my homework I have to feel right. After sitting on a hard chair all day, I need to stretch out with my head on a pillow. Mum says I cannot possibly concentrate like that, but actually I don't fall asleep as long as I don't go on too late, and I have the window open to get some fresh air. I'd love to work with music on, a lot of my friends do, and they say it really helps them concentrate. The point is I like music too much—it takes over from whatever I'm supposed to be doing.

Speaker 4

Boy: I'm hopeless at doing school projects. I make timetables so that I can complete the project well before the deadline, but I don't stick to them. I've tried everything—strong coffee, quiet rooms, fresh air. Even though I'm wide awake and there's nothing to disturb me, the work still doesn't get done. I was getting really worried last week, when Mary came round and asked if she could work in my room—hers is too dark and stuffy. I've never worked with a friend before and so I said 'No', but she was desperate. Eventually, I gave in and it really worked out for us both. I couldn't believe it!

Speaker 5

Girl: I really like some of the subjects I'm doing this year, particularly maths and physics. I don't mind studying them at all, although some of the homework assignments we're given are quite tricky, so I need to be able to work undisturbed. That's often a bit difficult in our house, unless I put it off until everyone's in bed. Did you know that my younger brother, Fred, plays the guitar in a band? I love some of their music, it's really cool, you'd love it too, but it's pointless trying to work when he's playing.

SECTION 3

▶ 听力原题

Part 3

You will hear five different people talking about hotels they have recently stayed with their children. For Questions 19–23, choose from the list (A–F) what each speaker says. Use the letters only once. There is one extra letter which you do not need to use.

A. Teenagers might not enjoy staying at this particular hotel.

B. The hotel was quite expensive.

C. A playground would have improved the facilities.

D. The hotel needed to know if you wanted your children to eat early.

E. There was no swimming pool available in the hotel.

F. Children under ten were not allowed to stay at the hotel.

Speaker 1	19
Speaker 2	20
Speaker 3	21
Speaker 4	22
Speaker 5	23

▶ 填空练习

Speaker 1

Woman: We chose this hotel because we knew that the _____ ____ _____ _____ of their own. The room _____ _____ _____ _____ _____ _____, but then it was _____ _____. They _____ ___ ____ _____ if you told them in good time, so that the _____ _____ _____ ____ _____ later in the _____ _____ _____. There were _____ ____ _____ for the children to play with, ____ _____ _____ with a _____, _____ and a _____. We _____ _____ our two all week.

Speaker 2

Man: We always _____ _____ _____ _____ which _____ _____ _____. This one was _____ _____ because the bedroom had a _____ _____ room, so we _____ all _____ together in one room. Although it wasn't the _____ _____, far from it in fact, it was _____ it. Our teenage kids loved the _____ _____ _____ _____ and the _____ _____, which were _____ _____ by the hotel. _____, the owners' kids, who've _____ _____ and left home now, _____ _____ _____ _____ _____. There was also an _____ ____ _____. Another thing we liked was the separate dining room for people with young families.

Speaker 3

Woman: We'd had a _____ _____ the year before at a hotel which didn't _____ _____ children. But this year we _____ _____ _____ _____ _____ _____ of the hotel. The rooms were _____ _____ _____ _____ four beds _____, and there was an _____ _____ in the garden for the _____ _____. You don't have to _____ _____ _____ _____ ten _____ the room—even meals were free for them, so that was another _____. There was lots to do _____ _____ _____ and tennis. But if you wanted to swim, you had to go to the _____ _____ _____, which the kids loved.

Speaker 4

Man: In the hotel we went to, we had a family _____ which was very _____. There was an _____ _____ _____ and _____ _____, so the kids _____ _____ _____ _____ _____ in the pool. _____ _____ _____ _____ children like swimming you're alright 'cos there wasn't much else for them to do. I did think that they _____ _____ _____ in a playground too. Young children under ten _____ _____ in the _____ _____ but there was an _____ _____ for them. This meant that we could have a quiet dinner for two when they were in bed.

Speaker 5

Woman: What we liked about our hotel was its size. It was only a small hotel and we _____ _____ _____ like family. The room had _____ _____ _____ _____, _____ toys and books, which the children loved. The guest _____ and _____ was a _____ _____ after seven thirty which _____ us fine 'cos there was a _____ children's supper at six, which _____ that they could go to bed _____ and get a good _____ _____. Older children aren't _____ _____ _____ and this hotel is _____ _____ for those with younger kids.

▶ 听力原文

Speaker 1

Woman: We chose this hotel because we knew that the owners had young children of their own. The room could have been a bit bigger, but then it was quite inexpensive. They provided an early supper if you told them in good time, so that the parents could eat in peace later in the cosy dining room. There were hundreds of toys for the children to play with, a huge garden with a playground, ponds and a playhouse. We hardly saw our two all week.

Speaker 2

Man: We always have difficulty finding hotels which welcome our children. This one was particularly good because the bedroom had a separate sitting room, so we weren't all squashed together in one room. Although it wasn't the cheapest around, far from it in fact, it was worth it. Our teenage kids loved the outdoor heated swimming pool and the mountain bikes, which were provided free by the hotel. Apparently, the owners' kids, who've grown up and left home now, had been mad on mountain biking. There was also an all-weather tennis court. Another thing we liked was the separate dining room for people with young families.

Speaker 3

Woman: We'd had a bad experience the year before at a hotel which didn't cater for children. But this year we were very impressed by the hospitality of the hotel. The rooms were large enough to accommodate four beds comfortably, and there was an adventure playground in the garden for the younger kids. You don't have to pay for children under ten sharing the room—even meals were free for them, so that was another bonus. There was lots to do including horse riding and tennis. But if you wanted to swim, you had to go to the local leisure centre, which the kids loved.

Speaker 4

Man: In the hotel we went to, we had a family suite which was very spacious. There was an outdoor heated pool and large grounds, so the kids spent most of the time in the pool. So long as your children like swimming you're alright 'cos there wasn't much else for them to do. I did think that they could have put in a playground too. Young children under ten aren't allowed in the dining room but there was an early supper for them. This meant that we could have a quiet dinner for two when they were in bed.

Speaker 5

Woman: What we liked about our hotel was its size. It was only a small hotel and we were looked after like family. The room had loads of soft toys, wooden toys and books, which the children loved. The guest lounge and conservatory was a child-free zone after seven thirty which suited us fine 'cos there was a special children's supper at six, which meant that they could go to bed early and get a good night's sleep. Older children aren't really catered for and this hotel is probably better for those with younger kids.

SECTION 4

▶ 听力原题

Part 3

You will hear five different cyclists talking about a long-distance race they took part in. For Questions 19–23, choose from the list (A–F) what each speaker says. Use the letters only once. There is one extra letter which you do not need to use.

A. I started the race but then decided not to continue.

B. I had to change bicycles during the race.

C. I felt uncomfortable on my bicycle throughout the race.

D. I had done some serious physical training for the race.

E. I think the organisers of the race were inefficient.

F. I was satisfied with my performance in the race.

Speaker 1		19
Speaker 2		20
Speaker 3		21
Speaker 4		22
Speaker 5		23

▶ 填空练习

Speaker 1

Woman: This was my first _____ _____ _____ the really _____ _____. When you _____ ___ _____ _____ _____ _____ _____, it's hard to find an easy _____ _____, and as a result, you get ___ _____ _____ in your back. You can _____ _____ ____ _____ _____, and that sometimes helps. But it didn't with me. ____ ____ _____, I found myself _____ _____ _____ _____ _____ ___ _____ _____, _____ ___ _____ _____, luckily. If the bike had been _____ I'd _____ _____ then and there, but it was OK. I _____ ___ to the end but the _____ _____ in my back didn't get any better.

Speaker 2

Man: We _____ _____ towns and also through _____ _____, and everything was _____ until I _____ __ ___ _____ ___. I knew I had an _____ here, because I'm _____ ___ _____ ___ _____. No _____ _____ for me! But at some point, _____ ____ _____, I _____ _____ __ __ _____ _____ _____. I'd been told before the start that there'd be a _____ _____, so even if your bike broke down, they'd be there to help you _____. Well, they _____ _____ _____ ___ _____ things _____ because I had to wait far too long, and so was one of the last _____ to ___ the _____ _____.

Speaker 3

Man: I'd ＿＿＿ ＿＿＿＿＿ ＿＿＿ all the ＿＿＿＿＿ ＿＿＿＿ of the race, and so it ＿＿＿＿＿ ＿＿ ＿＿＿＿ ＿＿＿＿ ＿＿＿ ＿＿＿ ＿＿＿. However, ＿＿＿＿ through, I ＿＿＿＿ my ＿＿＿ ＿＿＿＿＿ was to ＿＿＿ ＿＿＿. I hadn't done ＿＿＿＿＿ ＿＿＿＿＿. In a race like that, you need to ＿＿＿＿＿ ＿＿ ＿＿＿＿＿ ＿＿＿＿＿, even when you are going up what looks like a ＿＿＿＿＿＿＿. If you are not ＿＿＿ ＿＿＿＿＿, your leg ＿＿＿＿＿＿ may seem to ＿＿＿＿ ＿＿＿ ＿＿＿＿＿ ＿＿＿ ＿＿＿＿＿＿＿ ＿＿＿! I saw other riders ＿＿＿＿＿ ＿＿＿ me—I couldn't believe it. ＿＿＿＿＿, I thought, this is ＿＿＿＿＿, I may ＿＿＿ ＿＿ ＿＿＿ a ＿＿＿ ＿＿＿＿＿＿, so that was that.

Speaker 4

Woman: Well, I think I was ＿＿＿＿ ＿＿＿＿＿＿＿ ＿＿＿＿＿＿＿. I came up this village road and there were all these cars ＿＿＿＿＿＿＿＿＿ ＿＿＿＿＿＿ ＿＿＿＿＿＿. There had been an ＿＿＿＿＿ ＿＿＿ ＿＿＿＿＿＿＿. Anyway, it was ＿＿＿＿＿＿ ＿＿＿ ＿＿＿＿＿＿ them, on such a ＿＿＿＿＿ ＿＿＿, so they ＿＿＿＿＿ ＿＿ ＿＿＿＿. I'm ＿＿＿＿＿ with what I've ＿＿＿＿＿＿, although I didn't ＿＿＿＿＿ any of the ＿＿＿＿＿. ＿＿＿＿＿＿, I ＿＿＿＿＿＿ all the ＿＿＿＿＿＿ bits of the ＿＿＿＿＿, and I know that if it ＿＿＿＿＿ ＿＿＿ ＿＿＿ ＿＿＿ ＿＿＿＿＿, I would have ＿＿＿＿＿ ＿＿＿ ＿＿＿＿＿ ＿＿＿＿＿ ＿＿＿＿＿＿＿. Also my bike was great—I'd had it ＿＿＿＿＿＿ ＿＿＿＿＿＿＿ and wasn't sure it ＿＿＿＿＿ ＿＿＿＿＿＿ this test.

Speaker 5

Man: I have lots of ＿＿＿＿＿＿＿ ＿＿＿＿＿＿＿, but I knew this was going to be a long race, and your ＿＿＿＿＿＿ can get very ＿＿＿＿＿ and ＿＿＿＿＿＿. But I was ＿＿＿＿＿＿ ＿＿＿＿ ＿＿＿ ＿＿＿＿＿＿, after ＿＿＿＿＿＿ of ＿＿＿＿＿＿＿＿＿ to ＿＿＿＿＿ ＿＿＿ ＿＿＿＿＿. In fact, I could almost say I ＿＿＿＿ it, because I ＿＿＿＿＿＿＿ ＿＿＿ ＿＿＿＿＿ ＿＿＿＿ a couple of months before the race, which ＿＿＿＿＿＿ ＿＿＿ ＿＿＿＿ ＿＿＿＿＿＿. But I certainly wasn't ＿＿＿＿＿ my bike to ＿＿＿＿ ＿＿＿ ＿＿＿ ＿＿＿＿＿! But that's what happened unfortunately. I had ＿＿＿＿＿＿ ＿＿＿＿ ＿＿＿＿ ＿＿＿＿＿＿＿＿＿ ＿＿＿＿＿＿ ＿＿＿＿＿ ever, so it was all the more ＿＿＿＿＿＿＿＿ that it had to end like this.

▶ 听力原文

Speaker 1

Woman: This was my first bike ride across the really difficult ground. When you ride at speed on rough tracks, it's hard to find an easy riding position, and as a result, you get an unpleasant stiffness in your back. You can stand up on the bike, and that sometimes helps. But it didn't with me. On the contrary, I found myself flying over the handle bars a couple of times, landing on soft grass, luckily. If the bike had been damaged I'd have stopped then and there, but it was OK. I carried on to the end but the slight pain in my back didn't get any better.

Speaker 2

Man: We cycled through towns and also through remote areas, and everything was fine until I came to a hilly bit. I knew I had an advantage here, because I'm good at speeding up slopes. No aching muscles for me! But at some point, during the climb, I noticed one of the wheels needed adjusting. I'd been told before the start that there'd be a support team, so even if your bike broke down, they'd be there to help you immediately. Well, they certainly weren't capable of running things properly because I had to wait far too long, and so was one of the last competitors to reach the finishing line.

Speaker 3

Man: I'd been involved in all the planning stages of the race, and so it seemed a good idea to take part. However, halfway through, I realised my best option was to turn back. I hadn't done enough training. In a race like that, you need to keep a regular speed, even when you are going up what looks like a mountainside. If you are not fit enough, your leg muscles may seem to refuse to keep on pedalling hard! I saw other riders speeding past me— I couldn't believe it. Anyway, I thought, this is silly, I may end up with a torn muscle, so that was that.

Speaker 4

Woman: Well, I think I was just plain unlucky. I came up this village road and there were all these cars moving slowly uphill. There had been an accident or something. Anyway, it was impossible to overtake them, on such a narrow path, so they slowed me down. I'm content with what I've achieved, although I didn't win any of the prizes. Basically, I managed all the difficult bits of the race, and I know that if it hadn't been for that problem, I would have had a good chance of winning. Also my bike was great—I'd had it repaired recently and wasn't sure it would stand this test.

Speaker 5

Man: I have lots of cycling experience, but I knew this was going to be a long race, and your muscles can get very tired and strained. But I was ready for the challenge, after months of weightlifting to increase my strength. In fact, I could almost say I overdid it, because I developed an elbow problem a couple of months before the race, which fortunately was not serious. But I certainly wasn't expecting my bike to give me any trouble! But that's what happened unfortunately. I had started the race feeling fitter than ever, so it was all the more disappointing that it had to end like this.

CHAPTER 4   FCE LISTENING PART 4

FCE LISTENING

FCE LISTENING

FCE LISTENING

FCE LISTENING

FCE LISTENING

FCE LISTENING

FCE LISTENING

FCE LISTENING

SECTION 1

▶ 听力原题

Part 4

You will hear an interview with Trina Trevose, a pop singer who is only fifteen. For Questions 24–30, choose the best answer (A, B or C).

24　When Trina went to the USA, she

A. thought the records she made would be unsuccessful.

B. spent all her vacation making a record.

C. didn't tell many people why she was going.

25　When Trina was in the USA, she wrote songs about

A. her hometown.

B. the weather.

C. people she met.

26　Where was Trina performing when she was noticed by the record company?

A. in London

B. near her home

C. in a big city

27　Why did Trina sing with David Pearson?

A. He needed some help.

B. She is his fan.

C. The record company asked her to.

28　Trina was asked to return to the USA to

A. re-do some work.

B. act in some new films.

C. record a new song.

29　Why isn't Trina popular in Britain?

A. Her kind of music isn't popular in Britain.

B. She is constantly performing in the USA.

C. Her records haven't been available in Britain.

30   How does Trina see her future?

A. She will continue to perform in the USA.

B. She may make singing her career eventually.

C. She wants to study music at college.

▶ 填空练习

Interviewer: …Trina, you're 15 and you've just come back from America _____ _____ _____ _____ _____ . What ____ it _____?

Trina: It was wonderful. I had the six-week school summer holidays and, you know, went over there for a month, and then started school again.

Interviewer: What did your _____ ____ ____ ____?

Trina: I just told _____ friends what I was _____ in ____ _____… And I thought, well, if the _____ ____ _____, then I'd tell everyone…

Interviewer: And they were successful.

Trina: Right. And my friends were very good about it. Not _____, or anything.

Interviewer: Did you like being in the USA?

Trina: Oh, yes, most of the time it was great—the people are so _____.

Interviewer: Did you _____ ____ _____ ____ _____ there?

Trina: Well, yeah, I did. Most of the _____ I'd done in England _____ _____ about the people _____ to me—you know, Mum, Dad, my sister. They weren't with me in the States, and _____ I _____ them and _____ _____ like the rain in England and fish and chips, _____ _____ with new faces _____ ____ ____ ____ _____ ____ ____ _____.

Interviewer: Now, your home in England is a long way from London.

Trina: Yes, about ____ ____ ____ ____ ____ ____!

Interviewer: So, is it easy to get into the music _____ if you live that far away? Don't you have to be in London or near a big city at least?

Trina: No, no. We _____ _____ in London _____, but we were _____ _____ at a local concert, so I don't think it's _____ ____ _____ _____ anywhere. There are lots of _____ _____ _____ _____ bands, and they do go _____ ___ _____ _____ from the cities to find them. I was _____ _____ my band, and there have been other bands like us that've been lucky as well, so you don't have to come from a huge city _____ ____ _____.

Interviewer: Now, in the USA you did a song with someone who was a star when I ___ _____ _____, David Pearson, and you _____ ___ _____ _____ ___ _____?

Trina: No. It was _____, _____. But he was a really _____ ____. He was _____ ____ _____ in the same studio, and he had this song that he _____ _____ to sing with him, and he asked me, and I was only too _____ ____ ____ it!

Interviewer: But that wasn't the only _____ ____ you _____ with in the States, was it?

Trina: No, there was Lance Lakatoff.

Interviewer: But you _____ _____ ____ him...

Trina: Yes. He' s ___ _____ ___ ___ _____ ___ _____, in fact.

Interviewer: And you were in his TV _____?

Trina: Yes.

Interviewer: And what was that like?

Trina: It was a really good _____. I _____ _____ _____ ____ _____ _____. And they _____ us for three or four days, you know. That was the end of it. Or so I thought! But they had _____ some _____, which was ____ ___ _____, because I had to go back to the USA! I came home to England, and then they _____ ____ and said they had some bad camera work, etc., and I had to fly all the way back and do it again...

Interviewer: Actually, in the USA _____ _____ did well. But not here in England. Why's that?

Trina: Because you've never _____ ____ to ____ ___ _____ here in Britain. The record company's never _____ _____ _____ to ____ ____ _____ in _____, so it's always just been the USA, which is nice in a way.

Interviewer: Why do you say that?

Trina: Well, it's good to come home and ____ _____ _____ it.

Interviewer: But is it that the company don't think your _____ will _____ over here?

Trina: No, it's _____ the fact they don' t _____ over here. But the company's just _____ sold, and the new company does _____ over here, so maybe they will _____ ___ ____.

Interviewer: So, where do you see your _____ _____? Will you go back to the States?

Trina: Well, not for a while I shouldn't think, as I have another two years at school here in England. I know my _____ ___ _____ ___ _____, but I'm not sure that's for me, even to do music. Then, my _____ ____ _____ _____ ___ _____ ___ ___ ____ ___ ____ ____, and my parents say it's ___ ___ me, but I'm happy to wait a _____ _____ ____ _____. I can still write, after all—in fact one of my songs is in the American charts at the moment, but sung by someone else.

Interviewer: Well, the best of luck, Trina, and now…

▶ 听力原文

Interviewer: …Trina, you're 15 and you've just come back from America where you've been making records. What was it like?

Trina: It was wonderful. I had the six-week school summer holidays and, you know, went over there for a month, and then started school again.

Interviewer: What did your classmates at school think?

Trina: I just told close friends what I was doing in the States… And I thought, well, if the records were successful, then I'd tell everyone…

Interviewer: And they were successful.

Trina: Right. And my friends were very good about it. Not envious, or anything.

Interviewer: Did you like being in the USA?

Trina: Oh, yes, most of the time it was great—the people are so friendly.

Interviewer: Did you manage to write any songs there?

Trina: Well, yeah, I did. Most of the stuff I'd done in England had been about the people closest to me—you know, Mum, Dad, my sister. They weren't with me in the States, and although I missed them and silly things like the rain in England and fish and chips, being surrounded with new faces gave me lots of material for my songs.

Interviewer: Now, your home in England is a long way from London.

Trina: Yes, about as far as you can get!

Interviewer: So, is it easy to get into the music business if you live that far away? Don't you have to be in London or near a big city at least?

Trina: No, no. We did play in London once, but we were actually approached at a local concert, so I don t think it's impossible to get noticed anywhere. There are lots of record companies looking for bands, and they do go quite a long way from the cities to find them. I was lucky with my band, and there have been other bands like us that've been lucky as well, so you don't have to come from a huge city to be discovered.

Interviewer: Now, in the USA you did a song with someone who was a star when I was your age, David Pearson, and you hadn't any idea who he was?

Trina: No. It was embarrassing, actually. But he was a really pleasant guy. He was recording an album in the same studio, and he had this song that he needed someone to sing with him, and he asked me, and I was only too delighted to do it!

Interviewer: But that wasn't the only famous star you worked with in the States, was it?

Trina: No, there was Lance Lakatoff.

Interviewer: But you had heard of him…

Trina: Yes. He' s a bit of a hero of mine, in fact.

Interviewer: And you were in his TV series?

Trina: Yes.

Interviewer: And what was that like?

Trina: It was a really good experience. I hadn't done anything like that before. And they filmed us for three or four days, you know. That was the end of it. Or so I thought! But they had made some mistakes, which was such a shame, because I had to go back to the USA! I came home to England, and then they phoned up and said they had some bad camera work, etc., and I had to fly all the way back and do it again…

Interviewer: Actually, in the USA your record did well. But not here in England. Why's that?

Trina: Because you've never been able to get it over here in Britain. The record company's never had any arrangements to sell their records in Britain, so it's always just been the USA, which is nice in a way.

Interviewer: Why do you say that?

Trina: Well, it's good to come home and get away from it.

Interviewer: But is it that the company don't think your style will appeal over here?

Trina: No, it's purely the fact they don't operate over here. But the company's just been sold, and the new company does operate over here, so maybe they will release the record.

Interviewer: So, where do you see your career going? Will you go back to the States?

Trina: Well, not for a while I shouldn't think, as I have another two years at school here in England. I know my schoolfriends are thinking of college, but I'm not sure that's for me, even to do music. Then, my agent has been trying to persuade me to do it full time, and my parents say it's up to me, but I'm happy to wait a while before that happens. I can still write, after all—in fact one of my songs is in the American charts at the moment, but sung by someone else.

Interviewer: Well, the best of luck, Trina, and now…

SECTION 2

▶ 听力原题

Part 4

You will hear a girl called Tricia Simpkins talking at a public meeting about a plan to create a nature reserve in the centre of a large city. For Questions 24–30, choose the best answer (A, B or C).

---

24   How did Tricia once feel about the countryside?

  A. She enjoyed rural life.

  B. She paid no attention to it.

  C. She wanted others to experience it.

25   Why did Tricia take part in a wildlife survey?

  A. She was required to do it.

  B. She was interested in wildlife.

  C. She was asked to do it by her neighbours.

26   What does Tricia say about the results of the survey?

  A. They are disappointing.

  B. They are confusing.

  C. They are unexpected.

27   What does Tricia say about the problems created by trees?

  A. People exaggerate them.

  B. People neglect them.

  C. People accept them.

28   According to Tricia, what is wrong with the trees the council is planting?

  A. They are too costly to replace.

  B. They fail to attract wildlife.

  C. They are too small for the area.

29   What used to happen in the wasteland at the end of Tricia's street?

  A. People used to walk their dogs there.

  B. People used to leave rubbish there.

  C. Children used to play there.

30   What is Tricia's suggestion for the new nature reserve?

A. to allow the planting of trees

B. to build some recreational facilities

C. to let it go wild

▶ 填空练习

Man: Good afternoon. Thank you for coming to this _____ _____ which ____ _____

_____ ____ _____ the idea of _____ ____ _____ _____ in the city—that is, an

area where _____ ____ _____, and to begin with, local teenager, Tricia Simpkins,

is going to tell us some of the _____ ___ the idea. Tricia.

Tricia: Yes. Hello…I'd like to _____ ___ _____ that, like many city teenagers, I don't _____

_____ _____ with the _____. I live ____ a _____, _____ _____ _____,

full of people and cars, in the middle of a _____ ____, and I'd never _____ _____

_____ to wildlife. Even though every house down my street has got a bit of a garden

and we have trees _____ ____ _____ and __ _____ ___ _____ _____ at one

end, it _____ _____ ____ ___ __ ___ _____, and I took it all ____ _____.

My _____ _____ to _____ when we had to do a _____ ___ ____ _____ in the

city as part of a school project. We chose ten families from the street and we asked them

just to _____ _____ ____ ___ _____, _____, _____ and so on that they could

_____ _____ in their garden or down the street _____ ___ ____ _____ ___

_____.

All sorts of _____ _____ soon _____ _____ ___ ___ ___ _____, like that

we have twenty different sorts of _____, fifty different _____ ____ ____, and all sorts

of animals, even some quite large ones like foxes and deer. At first we _____ what it

_____, like was it a _____ _____ or something? We'd no way of knowing. So what we

did, we got in _____ ____ a _____ _____ out in the country, and asked them what

you could see there. And that's when we _____ that we've as much, if not more _____

_____ they do. And that's what really got us _____ ____ ___ ____ of a _____

_____ here.

Because what _____ ____ now is that we ____ ___ _____ our _____ _____.
One _____ _____ thing ____ _____ all the _____ ____ of trees in the
streets. We've got really big old trees here in this part of the city, and of course if one
_____ _____ in a storm or gets a _____, it has to be _____. But this year alone,
over one hundred of these trees _____ _____ _____ ____. Now the reason _____ for
this is that the trees have really _____ _____ _____ which makes it _____ for
people _____ ___ _____, _____ _____ and things. But we think these problems are
not as _____ as they are _____ out to be, and there's no _____ for all this _____.

What's more, although the _____ _____ has _____ to ____ ____ _____ ___ _____
___ the old ones, what they're planting are these little _____ ____ that look nice, but
the birds and animals just don't use them in the same way. And they're not even _____
_____, because more suitable trees cost just the same.

Another example of what can happen is the _____ at the end of our street. It _____
____ the _____ _____ and as children we all _____ to ____ there and we thought it
was _____ great _____. it was so _____ in _____ and wild flowers that you could
get _____ if you went off the little _____ _____. Then, a few years ago, no _____
_____ they were doing the right thing, the council _____ to ____ it _____. Now
it's just an area of grass where people go to _____ ____ _____. There are a few little
trees, but _____ there's ___ ___ ____ there ____ _____.

So, what I'd like to _____ _____ _____ ____ ____ we use this ____ to ____ a _____
_____. We think it should be _____ ____ go back to its _____ _____, ____
_____ ___ ____ for the ____ ____ which may be _____ from the loss of trees in the
area. This would, of course, also be a ____ ____ for people who want to ___ _____ ____
the _____ of ___ ____, which is _____ something we would want to _____ _____.

So, I would like you…

▶ 听力原文

Man:　Good afternoon. Thank you for coming to this public meeting which has been called to discuss the idea of creating a nature reserve in the city—that is, an area where wildlife is protected, and to begin with, local teenager, Tricia Simpkins, is going to tell us some of the background to the idea. Tricia.

Tricia: Yes. Hello…I'd like to start by saying that, like many city teenagers, I don't have much contact with the countryside. I live off a busy, polluted shopping street, full of people and cars, in the middle of a crowded city, and I'd never given any thought to wildlife. Even though every house down my street has got a bit of a garden and we have trees along the road and a piece of waste ground at one end, it seemed nothing out of the ordinary, and I took it all for granted.

My attitude started to change when we had to do a survey of the wildlife in the city as part of a school project. We chose ten families from the street and we asked them just to write down all the animals, birds, insects and so on that they could remember seeing in their garden or down the street during the last couple of years.

All sorts of surprising things soon started coming out of that survey, like that we have twenty different sorts of butterfly, fifty different types of birds, and all sorts of animals, even some quite large ones like foxes and deer. At first we wondered what it meant, like was it a world record or something? We'd no way of knowing. So what we did, we got in touch with a nature reserve out in the country, and asked them what you could see there. And that's when we realised that we've as much, if not more wildlife than they do. And that's what really got us interested in the idea of a nature reserve here.

Because what worries us now is that we may be losing our local wildlife. One specially worrying thing has been all the cutting down of trees in the streets. We've got really big old trees here in this part of the city, and of course if one gets damaged in a storm or gets a disease, it has to be removed. But this year alone, over one hundred of these trees have been chopped down. Now the reason given for this is that the trees have really extensive root systems which makes it difficult for people laying gas pipes, electricity cables and things. But we think these problems are not as serious as they are made out to be, and there's no need for all this destruction.

What's more, although the local council has agreed to plant new trees in place of the old ones, what they're planting are these little ornamental trees that look nice, but the birds and animals just don't use them in the same way. And they're not even saving money, because more suitable trees cost just the same.

Another example of what can happen is the wasteland at the end of our street. It belongs to the city council and as children we all used to play there and we thought it was really great because it was so covered in bushes and wild flowers that you could get lost if you went off the little muddy tracks. Then, a few years ago, no doubt thinking they were doing the right thing, the council decided to tidy it up. Now it's just an area of grass where people go to exercise their dogs. There are a few little trees, but basically there's not a lot there any more.

So, what I'd like to propose this afternoon is that we use this space to create a nature reserve. We think it should be allowed to go back to its natural condition, thus providing a refuge for the local wildlife which may be suffering from the loss of trees in the area. This would, of course, also be a leisure amenity for people who want to get away from the stresses of city living, which is hardly something we would want to deny them.

So, I would like you...

SECTION 3

▶ 听力原题

Part 4

You will hear a radio interview with a young tennis player, Alice Winters, and her coach, Bruce Gray. For Questions 24–30, choose the best answer (A, B or C).

24　What does Bruce say about getting financial help?

　　A. He finds it is hard to obtain any.

　　B. He expects that they will get some soon.

　　C. He thinks they can succeed without it.

25　What is Alice's attitude towards training?

　　A. She wants a better training condition.

　　B. She wishes she had more time for other things.

　　C. She sometimes finds it hard to make the effort.

26　What is Alice's attitude towards her schoolwork?

　　A. She works hard to meet the requirement.

　　B. It is not the most important thing.

　　C. She is confident of her ability.

27　How does Alice feel about competitions?

　　A. The result is the most important thing.

　　B. She sometimes lacks confidence.

　　C. She always expects to win.

28　According to Bruce, what makes Alice exceptional?

　　A. her natural talent for the game

　　B. the time and effort she devotes

　　C. the way she reacts to other players

29　How does Alice feel about becoming a professional player?

　　A. She is looking forward to the glamorous lifestyle.

　　B. She realises she may not be successful.

　　C. She is worried about facing strong competitors.

30　How does Bruce describe Alice's character?

　　A. She is a very sociable person.

　　B. She is passionate and emotional.

　　C. She is surprisingly mature.

▶ 填空练习

Presenter:　In some sports, the players ＿＿＿＿ ＿＿ ＿＿ ＿＿＿＿ ＿＿＿＿ ＿＿ ＿＿＿＿. My guests today are 14-year-old Alice Winters, and her coach, Bruce Gray. Alice, as National Junior Tennis Champion, ＿＿ ＿＿＿ ＿＿＿＿ ＿＿＿ 'the most ＿＿＿＿ young player ＿＿＿ ＿＿＿＿'. Alice, Bruce, welcome.

Alice/Bruce:　Hello.

Presenter:　Let's start by ＿＿＿＿ ＿＿ ＿＿＿＿. Have you found it easy to ＿＿＿ ＿＿ ＿＿ ＿＿＿ ＿＿＿＿, Bruce?

Bruce:　Not really. We've ＿＿＿＿＿ ＿＿ ＿＿＿ ＿＿＿＿ ＿＿＿ ＿＿＿＿, but they ＿＿＿＿ ＿＿＿＿ ＿＿ their money ＿＿＿ something which ＿＿＿ ＿＿ ＿＿＿＿＿—Alice isn't that ＿＿＿ ＿＿＿ yet. So we'll ＿＿＿ ＿＿ ＿＿ ＿＿＿ ＿＿＿ it. And I ＿＿＿＿ that, with Alice's talent, there's no ＿＿＿＿ why we can't. That'd be an ＿＿＿＿ ＿＿＿＿ ＿＿＿＿, ＿＿＿＿ it?

Presenter:　Now Alice, you must do a lot of ＿＿＿＿＿? Is it sometimes a bit too ＿＿＿＿＿ ＿＿ ＿＿＿＿ ＿＿＿ your age?

Alice:　Well, a lot of ＿＿＿＿ ＿＿＿ age might ask themselves, 'Why can't I be like everyone else?', you know, ＿＿＿ in the ＿＿＿ and ＿＿ ＿＿＿＿, but that side of it doesn't ＿＿＿ ＿＿. I must ＿＿＿ though that there are ＿＿＿ when I just don't ＿＿＿ it—you know, ＿＿＿＿ ＿＿ ＿＿＿ ＿＿＿ when Bruce ＿＿＿ ＿＿＿ to take me on a ＿＿＿＿ ＿＿＿ and I think, 'Oh go away and ＿＿＿ ＿＿ ＿＿＿!' But ＿＿＿ ＿＿＿ that, well, I do it because I enjoy it. Nobody's ＿＿＿＿ me do it, are they? So I don't really see it as ＿＿＿ ＿＿＿＿.

Presenter:　And what about your ＿＿＿＿?

Alice:　Well, I'm ＿＿＿＿ ＿＿ ＿＿＿ ＿＿ ＿＿＿ at the moment, although I can see that if I do get ＿＿＿ ＿＿＿＿ the sport might get in the way of ＿＿＿ ＿＿＿, but, well, I know which comes first for me. After all, if I make it to the top in tennis, I won't ＿＿＿ ＿＿ ＿＿＿ ＿＿＿＿.

Presenter: Now Alice, when you're _____ ____ ___ _____, is it all _____ _____ or do you have fun?

Alice: Well, I'm only there for one reason really. I mean, I can't see the _____ _____. I'm not one of those people who think that _____ _____ _____ _____ ____ _____. I mean, I know I can't win every time, _____ ____ _____ people a lot older than me, but that's always the aim. And if I lose, well, I look at my _____ with Bruce, look at ways of _____ it, and well, I don't let it get to me. I'm just _____ _____ next time.

Presenter: Bruce, what do you think _____ Alice _____ _____ _____ _____ ____ ____ _____ ____?

Bruce: I've never _____ _____ any young player quite like her in all my years as a coach. What _____ _____ is—you can watch her play and she doesn't _____ ____ ____ _____, even though of course she is. With other players you can see the _____ _____ but with her, well, she's just so _____.

Presenter: So Alice, how do you ____ _____ _____?

Alice: Well, I'd love to _____ _____, but it's a bit early to _____ _____ about that. I mean, I'm a big fish in a _____ _____ at the moment, but as I get older, well, there are going to be a lot of _____ _____ out there. If I ____ ____ ____ _____ it full time…the _____ ____ _____ from outside, but it might just be too hard for me and I might _____ ____ ____ _____. But it's hard to say. Some people stay at the top for years, don't they?

Presenter: Bruce, do you and Alice ____ ____ _____? Is she an easy person to coach?

Bruce: You know, sometimes I find it _____ ____ _____ ____ _____ she is because she's got an _____ _____ ____ _____ _____. We've had the _____…shall I say…_____ but she _____ _____ _____ _____ _____ _____, it soon passes. She doesn't have a _____ _____ to say, I guess, when we're working or travelling to tournaments. She has friends outside the game, but she doesn't have _____ _____ for a _____ _____ at the moment.

Presenter: Well, Alice and Bruce, _____ ____ _____ my guests and good luck for the future.

Alice/Bruce: Thank you.

▶ 听力原文

Presenter:	In some sports, the players seem to be getting younger and younger. My guests today are 14-year-old Alice Winters, and her coach, Bruce Gray. Alice, as National Junior Tennis Champion, has been described as 'the most talented young player for years'. Alice, Bruce, welcome.
Alice/Bruce:	Hello.
Presenter:	Let's start by talking about money. Have you found it easy to get help in that respect, Bruce?
Bruce:	Not really. We've applied to local companies for sponsorship, but they would sooner put their money into something which gets them publicity—Alice isn't that well known yet. So we'll probably have to get there without it. And I reckon that, with Alice's talent, there's no reason why we can't. That'd be an even greater achievement, wouldn't it?
Presenter:	Now Alice, you must do a lot of training? Is it sometimes a bit too demanding for someone of your age?
Alice:	Well, a lot of players my age might ask themselves, 'Why can't I be like everyone else?', you know, free in the evenings and at weekends, but that side of it doesn't bother me. I must admit though that there are times when I just don't fancy it—you know, freezing cold winter mornings when Bruce comes round to take me on a training run and I think, 'Oh go away and leave me alone!' But apart from that, well, I do it because I enjoy it. Nobody's making me do it, are they? So I don't really see it as making sacrifices.
Presenter:	And what about your schoolwork?
Alice:	Well, I'm managing to keep up with at the moment, although I can see that if I do get more successful the sport might get in the way of academic work, but, well, I know which comes first for me. After all, if I make it to the top in tennis, I won't need any academic qualifications.
Presenter:	Now Alice, when you're competing in a tournament, is it all terribly serious or do you have fun?
Alice:	Well, I'm only there for one reason really. I mean, I can't see the point otherwise. I'm not one of those people who think that taking part matters more than winning. I mean, I know I can't win every time, especially up against people a lot older than me, but that's always the aim. And if I lose, well, I look at my performance with Bruce, look at ways of improving it, and well, I don't let it get to me. I'm just more determined next time.

Presenter: Bruce, what do you think makes Alice different from other players of the same age?

Bruce: I've never come across any young player quite like her in all my years as a coach. What amazes me is—you can watch her play and she doesn't seem to be trying, even though of course she is. With other players you can see the effort involved but with her, well, she's just so gifted.

Presenter: So Alice, how do you see your future?

Alice: Well, I'd love to turn professional, but it's a bit early to think seriously about that. I mean, I'm a big fish in a small pond at the moment, but as I get older, well, there are going to be a lot of tough players out there. If I do end up doing it full time…the lifestyle looks glamorous from outside, but it might just be too hard for me and I might decide to get out. But it's hard to say. Some people stay at the top for years, don't they?

Presenter: Bruce, do you and Alice get on well? Is she an easy person to coach?

Bruce: You know, sometimes I find it difficult to remember how young she is because she's got an old head on young shoulders. We've had the odd…shall I say…disagreement but she doesn't have much of a temper, it soon passes. She doesn't have a great deal to say, I guess, when we're working or travelling to tournaments. She has friends outside the game, but she doesn't have much time for a social life at the moment.

Presenter: Well, Alice and Bruce, thanks for being my guests and good luck for the future.

Alice/Bruce: Thank you.

SECTION 4

▶ 听力原题

Part 4

You will hear an interview with a TV presenter, Tanya Edwards, who is talking about her career and her daughter called Maddy. For Questions 24–30, choose the best answer (A, B or C).

24　What does Tanya say about her first job in children's TV?

　　A. She had contacted the TV company earlier.

　　B. She found this job very rewarding.

　　C. Her previous experience was useful.

25　What does Tanya say about Paul Broadly, her first boss?

　　A. He thought of nothing but his work.

　　B. He made decisions on his own.

　　C. He was unwilling to share ideas about the work.

26　What does Tanya say about her parachute jump?

　　A. She feels a little uneasy afterward.

　　B. It resulted in unexpected attention.

　　C. Her boss was cross about what happened.

27　What does Tanya say about her daughter's flute playing?

　　A. She realised that Maddy had some gifts.

　　B. She saw that Maddy liked an audience.

　　C. She wanted Maddy to practise more.

28　How does Tanya feel when her daughter sings in public?

　　A. responsible for Maddy's success

　　B. recognised the importance of professional guidance

　　C. aware of how the audience feels

29　Tanya says that Maddy finds modelling difficult because

　　A. she questions her own beauty.

　　B. you have to cope with criticism.

　　C. people don't respect models.

30　What is Tanya's attitude to fame in general?

　　A. You should enjoy it while it lasts.

　　B. You should ignore other people's attitudes.

　　C. You should accept its drawbacks.

▶ 填空练习

Interviewer: Today, in our series about _____ _____, the TV _____, Tanya Edwards, talks about her first job and also about her daughter, Maddy, a pop star and _____. Tanya, your first job was in _____ _____, _____ it?

Tanya: When I was _____ _____ for a job _____ ___ _____ television, I didn't want to do the job at all. I'd always _____ ___ ___ ___ _____, and had done a lot of _____ ___ _____. In fact, it was the _____ _____ to _____ that I _____ _____ _____ _____, because it was _____ a live programme—so having been ____ _____ ____ _____ _____ ___ ___ _____. In those days, we didn't have _____—you know, that's where you have a little _____ _____ ___ _____ ____, and you can hear the _____ _____ to you—so we had to _____ ___ _____ _____ ___ ___ _____…which worked fine.

Interviewer: You had an _____ ____, ____ you?

Tanya: Yes. Paul Broadly. He was a very _____ programme _____. He _____ ___ ____ _____. He _____ quite old to me when I started—he was a grandfather—but he had this ____ ___ _____ what children could enjoy watching. He was _____ _____ to _____ the best children's television—whether it was something about _____ ___ _____, or how to _____ ___ _____ ____. He was _____ to the programme, _____ _____ about it, and _____ ___ ___ ____ _____ ___ _____.

Interviewer: But you enjoyed it?

Tanya: Oh, yes, and there was always something different. I even did _____ for the programme. There I was, _____ ____ ___ this _____, with the cameras on me—trying to smile, although it was _____ _____! The _____ _____ was that the _____ _____ _____, but I ____ ___ _____ _____ ___ the car, _____ the _____— and broke my _____. I thought my boss would be _____, but in fact he was okay about it, and I was _____ that lots of the children who watched the programme _____ ___ _____—one even sent me a cake.

Interviewer: And your daughter is Maddy, the singer and model. Did she always want to be famous?

Tanya: Well, we always had a lot of music in the house, when she was young. I wouldn't say that I knew that she would do _____ _____—I had to _____ her to learn an _____—but I ____ _____ one day, she was _____ ___ ___ doing her homework, and my husband _____ _____ the road and there was Maddy leaning out of the window, playing her _____ for all she was _____. It was a nice _____ day, and people were stopping and listening, and Maddy was _____ and really _____ ____ _____!

Interviewer: And she still does?

Tanya: Well, these days, years later, when I watch my daughter _____ in front of a big _____, there's always this _____ thing—I _____ ____ that _____ everyone is thinking that she's brilliant—it's not just me thinking, 'That's my little girl'— it's the whole room _____ _____ _____. It's not all roses, though. When Maddy had a bad _____ with her _____ _____, she was _____ ____ by a _____ _____.

Interviewer: Another _____ job.

Tanya: Well, I don't think that modelling's at all easy. And I know she finds it hard when people back at the _____ don't think she looks _____ ___ a _____ job—you know she's too tall or something, or not young enough. It can be hard—even if, like Maddy, you know you're beautiful.

Interviewer: Mm, and how do you both _____ _____ your _____?

Tanya: Well, we've talked about it—there is a _____ _____ that people get on their faces when they _____ you, and I think probably that that's what some people miss when they're __ _____ _____. But it also means that you can't go to the shops __ _____. And that can be tough—so is reading about yourself in the paper, when what's being said is __ _____ __ _____, but you just have to learn to _____ _____ that side of it…

▶ 听力原文

Interviewer: Today, in our series about celebrity families, the TV presenter, Tanya Edwards, talks about her first job and also about her daughter, Maddy, a pop star and model. Tanya, your first job was in children's television, wasn't it?

Tanya: When I was asked to audition for a job presenting on children's television, I didn't want to do the job at all. I'd always wanted to be an actress, and had done a lot of acting at college. In fact, it was the closest thing to acting that I could possibly have chosen, because it was presenting a live programme—so having been on stage in college productions came in handy. In those days, we didn't have talkback—you know, that's where you have a little gadget stuck in your ear, and you can hear the producer talking to you—so we had to rely on signals from the floor manager…which worked fine.

Interviewer: You had an extraordinary boss, didn't you?

Tanya: Yes. Paul Broadly. He was a very well-respected programme editor. He taught me so much. He seemed quite old to me when I started—he was a grandfather—but he had this way of understanding what children could enjoy watching. He was absolutely determined to produce the best children's television—whether it was something about wildlife on safari, or how to make a chocolate cake. He was devoted to the programme, completely single-minded about it, and expected us to feel exactly the same.

Interviewer: But you enjoyed it?

Tanya: Oh, yes, and there was always something different. I even did parachuting for the programme. There I was, leaping out of this aeroplane, with the cameras on me—trying to smile, although it was pretty scary! The stupid thing was that the jump went fine, but I fell over running back to the car, carrying the parachute—and broke my ankle. I thought my boss would be furious, but in fact he was okay about it, and I was amazed that lots of the children who watched the programme sent me cards—one even sent me a cake.

Interviewer: And your daughter is Maddy, the singer and model. Did she always want to be famous?

Tanya: Well, we always had a lot of music in the house, when she was young. I wouldn't say that I knew that she would do something special—I had to persuade her to learn an instrument—but I do remember one day, she was supposed to be doing her homework, and my husband came down the road and there was Maddy leaning out of the window, playing her flute for all she was worth. It was a nice sunny day, and people were stopping and listening, and Maddy was bowing and really enjoying the attention!

Interviewer: And she still does?

Tanya: Well, these days, years later, when I watch my daughter singing in front of a big crowd, there's always this curious thing—I suddenly realise that practically everyone is thinking that she's brilliant—it's not just me thinking, 'That's my little girl'—it's the whole room sharing the experience. It's not all roses, though. When Maddy had a bad patch with her singing career, she was taken on by a modelling agency.

Interviewer: Another glamorous job.

Tanya: Well, I don't think that modelling's at all easy. And I know she finds it hard when people back at the agency don't think she looks right for a particular job—you know she's too tall or something, or not young enough. It can be hard—even if, like Maddy, you know you're beautiful.

Interviewer: Mm, and how do you both deal with your fame?

Tanya: Well, we've talked about it—there is a certain look that people get on their faces when they recognise you, and I think probably that that's what some people miss when they're no longer famous. But it also means that you can't go to the shops in peace. And that can be tough—so is reading about yourself in the paper, when what's being said is a load of rubbish, but you just have to learn to cope with that side of it...

FCE LISTENING

FCE LISTENING

FCE LISTENING

FCE LISTENING

FCE LISTENING

FCE LISTENING

FCE LISTENING

FCE LISTENING

FCE LISTENING

CHAPTER 1   FCE LISTENING PART 1

SECTION 1

1. B   2. C   3. C   4. B   5. A   6. B   7. C   8. A

SECTION 2

1. C   2. B   3. B   4. A   5. A   6. C   7. A   8. C

SECTION 3

1. B   2. A   3. C   4. C   5. C   6. B   7. B   8. B

SECTION 4

1. B   2. C   3. A   4. A   5. A   6. B   7. B   8. B

CHAPTER 2   FCE LISTENING PART 2

SECTION 1

9. travel agent('s)/travel agency   10. poster   11. Changes

12. (local) (African) farmers   13. three/3 weeks   14. motorbike/motorcycle

15. (the) (local) women   16. traffic (noise)   17. (pieces of) furniture   18. gardening

SECTION 2

9. National Museum   10. final/last   11. glass work/glass   12. industrial

13. gun   14. waiter   15. films/movies   16. computer company

17. metal   18. (old) maps

SECTION 3

9. woodwork   10. detective   11. (old) photos/photographs

12. theatre/theater   13. Japan (and) Canada   14. (an) electric light/ (a) light/(electric) lighting/lights

15. 140 cm(s)/one hundred (and) forty centimentres/centimeters   16. windows

17. paper   18. (of) (the) pollution

SECTION 4

9. composer   10. concert halls/concerts

11. 9500/nine and a half thousand/nine thousand five hundred   12. contacts

13. mending	14. wood	15. school/schoolroom	16. (small) museum
17. heating [bill(s)]	18. dry		

CHAPTER 3   FCE LISTENING PART 3

SECTION 1

19. E	20. A	21. D	22. B	23. F

SECTION 2

19. B	20. A	21. F	22. D	23. E

SECTION 3

19. D	20. B	21. E	22. C	23. A

SECTION 4

19. C	20. E	21. A	22. F	23. D

CHAPTER 4   FCE LISTENING PART 4

SECTION 1

24. C	25. C	26. B	27. A	28. A	29. C	30. B

SECTION 2

24. B	25. A	26. C	27. A	28. B	29. C	30. C

SECTION 3

24. C	25. C	26. B	27. A	28. A	29. B	30. C

SECTION 4

24. C	25. A	26. B	27. B	28. C	29. B	30. C

扫描二维码
输入封面防伪标涂层下的序列号
在线收听本书音频

FCE LISTENING

FCE LISTENING

FCE LISTENING

FCE LISTENING

FCE LISTENING

FCE LISTENING

FCE LISTENING

FCE LISTENING

FCE LISTENING

Common Instructions & Listening Task Vocabulary

These words appear frequently in exam instructions and listening tasks.

☐ listen   ['lɪs(ə)n]   *v.* 听

☐ respond   [rɪ'spɒnd]   *v.* 回应，回答

☐ identify   [aɪ'dentɪfaɪ]   *v.* 识别

☐ select   [sɪ'lekt]   *v.* 选择

☐ match   [mætʃ]   *v.* 匹配

☐ choose   [tʃuːz]   *v.* 选择

☐ compare   [kəm'peə(r)]   *v.* 比较

☐ contrast   [kən'trɑːst]   *v.* 对比

☐ analyse   ['ænəlaɪz]   *v.* 分析

☐ infer   [ɪn'fɜː(r)]   *v.* 推断

☐ interpret   [ɪn'tɜːprət]   *v.* 解释，口译

☐ summarise   ['sʌməraɪz]   *v.* 总结

☐ paraphrase   ['pærəfreɪz]   *v.* 释义，改述

☐ predict   [prɪ'dɪkt]   *v.* 预测

☐ describe   [dɪ'skraɪb]   *v.* 描述

☐ elaborate   [ɪ'læbəreɪt]   *v.* 详细说明

☐ clarify   ['klærəfaɪ]   *v.* 澄清，解释

☐ evaluate   [ɪ'væljʊeɪt]   *v.* 评估

☐ discuss   [dɪ'skʌs]   *v.* 讨论

☐ focus   ['fəʊkəs]   *v.* 关注   *n.* 重点

☐ highlight   ['haɪlaɪt]   *v./n.* 强调，突出

☐ emphasise   ['emfəsaɪz]   *v.* 强调

☐ outline   ['aʊtlaɪn]   *v.* 概述   *n.* 提纲

Academic & Lecture Vocabulary

These words commonly appear in lectures, discussions, and academic listening tasks.

☐ lecture	['lektʃə(r)]	n.	讲座，演讲
☐ seminar	['semɪnɑː(r)]	n.	研讨会
☐ tutorial	[tjuː'tɔːrɪəl]	n.	辅导课
☐ assignment	[ə'saɪnmənt]	n.	作业
☐ research	[rɪ'sɜːtʃ]	n./v.	研究
☐ thesis	['θiːsɪs]	n.	论文
☐ statistics	[stə'tɪstɪks]	n.	统计数据
☐ findings	['faɪndɪŋz]	n.	研究结果
☐ analyse	['ænəlaɪz]	v.	分析
☐ data	['deɪtə]	n.	数据
☐ conclusion	[kən'kluːʒn]	n.	结论
☐ argument	['ɑːgjʊmənt]	n.	论点，争论
☐ debate	[dɪ'beɪt]	n./v.	辩论，讨论
☐ hypothesis	[haɪ'pɒθəsɪs]	n.	假设
☐ methodology	[ˌmeθə'dɒlədʒɪ]	n.	研究方法
☐ analysis	[ə'næləsɪs]	n.	分析
☐ evaluate	[ɪ'væljʊeɪt]	v.	评估
☐ investigate	[ɪn'vestɪgeɪt]	v.	调查
☐ plagiarism	['pleɪdʒərɪzəm]	n.	剽窃，抄袭
☐ draft	[drɑːft]	n.	草稿，初稿
☐ revise	[rɪ'vaɪz]	v.	修改，复习
☐ submit	[səb'mɪt]	v.	提交
☐ curriculum	[kə'rɪkjələm]	n.	课程

Health & Medicine Vocabulary

☐ symptom	['sɪmptəm]	n.	症状
☐ diagnosis	[ˌdaɪəg'nəʊsɪs]	n.	诊断

☐ prescription	[prɪˈskrɪpʃn]	n.	处方
☐ treatment	[ˈtriːtmənt]	n.	治疗
☐ therapy	[ˈθerəpɪ]	n.	治疗
☐ physiotherapy	[ˌfɪzɪəʊˈθerəpɪ]	n.	物理治疗
☐ surgery	[ˈsɜːdʒərɪ]	n.	外科手术
☐ physician	[fɪˈzɪʃ(ə)n]	n.	内科医生
☐ specialist	[ˈspeʃəlɪst]	n.	专科医生
☐ emergency	[ɪˈmɜːdʒənsɪ]	n.	紧急情况
☐ vaccine	[ˈvæksiːn]	n.	疫苗
☐ immunisation	[ˌɪmjʊnaɪˈzeɪʃn]	n.	免疫接种
☐ infection	[ɪnˈfekʃ(ə)n]	n.	感染
☐ antibiotic	[ˌæntɪbaɪˈɒtɪk]	n.	抗生素
☐ allergy	[ˈælədʒɪ]	n.	过敏
☐ chronic	[ˈkrɒnɪk]	adj.	慢性的
☐ acute	[əˈkjuːt]	adj.	急性的
☐ diagnose	[ˈdaɪəgnəʊz]	v.	诊断
☐ recover	[rɪˈkʌvə(r)]	v.	恢复
☐ relapse	[rɪˈlæps]	v./n.	复发
☐ overdose	[ˈəʊvədəʊs]	n./v.	过量服药
☐ contagious	[kənˈteɪdʒəs]	adj.	传染性的
☐ rehabilitation	[ˌriːəˌbɪlɪˈteɪʃn]	n.	康复
☐ mental health			心理健康
☐ first aid			急救

Law & Crime Vocabulary

☐ attorney	[əˈtɜːnɪ]	n.	律师
☐ defendant	[dɪˈfendənt]	n.	被告
☐ plaintiff	[ˈpleɪntɪf]	n.	原告
☐ prosecutor	[ˈprɒsɪkjuːtə(r)]	n.	公诉人
☐ jury	[ˈdʒʊərɪ]	n.	陪审团

☐ verdict	['vɜːdɪkt]	n. 判决
☐ trial	['traɪəl]	n. 审判
☐ conviction	[kən'vɪkʃn]	n. 定罪
☐ acquittal	[ə'kwɪt(ə)l]	n. 无罪释放
☐ sentence	['sentəns]	n. 判刑
☐ parole	[pə'rəʊl]	n. 假释
☐ appeal	[ə'piːl]	n./v. 上诉
☐ crime scene		犯罪现场
☐ evidence	['evɪdəns]	n. 证据
☐ testimony	['testɪmənɪ]	n. 证词
☐ alibi	['æləbaɪ]	n. 不在场证明
☐ suspect	['sʌspekt, sə'spekt]	n. 嫌疑人 v. 怀疑
☐ arrest	[ə'rest]	v./n. 逮捕
☐ interrogate	[ɪn'terəgeɪt]	v. 审讯
☐ fraud	[frɔːd]	n. 诈骗
☐ bribery	['braɪbərɪ]	n. 贿赂
☐ theft	[θeft]	n. 偷窃
☐ burglary	['bɜːglərɪ]	n. 入室盗窃
☐ manslaughter	['mænslɔːtə(r)]	n. 过失杀人
☐ homicide	['hɒmɪsaɪd]	n. 谋杀

News & Media Vocabulary

☐ journalist	['dʒɜːnəlɪst]	n. 记者
☐ correspondent	[ˌkɒrə'spɒndənt]	n. 特派记者
☐ editor	['edɪtə(r)]	n. 编辑
☐ anchor	['æŋkə(r)]	n. 新闻主持人
☐ reporter	[rɪ'pɔːtə(r)]	n. 记者
☐ broadcast	['brɔːdkɑːst]	n./v. 广播，播报
☐ coverage	['kʌvərɪdʒ]	n. 报道范围
☐ headline	['hedlaɪn]	n. 头条新闻

☐ breaking news　　　　　　　　　　　　重大新闻

☐ press release　　　　　　　　　　　　新闻发布

☐ censorship　　　['sensəʃɪp]　　　　*n.* 审查制度

☐ bias　　　　　　['baɪəs]　　　　　　*n.* 偏见

☐ propaganda　　[ˌprɒpə'gændə]　　*n.* 宣传

☐ interview　　　　['ɪntəvjuː]　　　　*n./v.* 采访

☐ quote　　　　　[kwəʊt]　　　　　　*n./v.* 引述，引用

☐ source　　　　　[sɔːs]　　　　　　　*n.* 消息来源

☐ feature article　　　　　　　　　　　专题报道

☐ press conference　　　　　　　　　　新闻发布会

☐ tabloid　　　　　['tæblɔɪd]　　　　　*n.* 小报

☐ circulation　　[ˌsɜːkjə'leɪʃ(ə)n]　*n.* 发行量

Travel & Directions Vocabulary

These words frequently appear in airport announcements, hotel bookings, and navigation-related listening tasks.

☐ accommodation　[əˌkɒmə'deɪʃ(ə)n]　*n.* 住宿

☐ itinerary　　　　[aɪ'tɪnərərɪ]　　　*n.* 旅行日程

☐ destination　　[ˌdestɪ'neɪʃn]　　　*n.* 目的地

☐ sightseeing　　['saɪtsiːɪŋ]　　　　*n.* 观光

☐ tourist attraction　　　　　　　　　旅游景点

☐ round trip　　　　　　　　　　　　　往返旅行

☐ departure　　　[dɪ'pɑːtʃə(r)]　　　*n.* 出发

☐ arrival　　　　　[ə'raɪv(ə)l]　　　　*n.* 到达

☐ baggage　　　　['bægɪdʒ]　　　　　*n.* 行李

☐ boarding pass　　　　　　　　　　　登机牌

☐ check-in counter　　　　　　　　　　值机柜台

☐ passport control　　　　　　　　　　护照检查

☐ customs declaration　　　　　　　　海关申报

☐ fare　　　　　　[feə(r)]　　　　　　*n.* 票价

☐ delay	[dɪˈleɪ]	*n./v.*	延误，推迟
☐ cancel	[ˈkæns(ə)l]	*v.*	取消
☐ commute	[kəˈmjuːt]	*v.*	通勤
☐ transfer	[trænsˈfɜː(r), ˈtrænfɜː(r)]	*v./n.*	转乘，换乘
☐ direct flight			直飞航班
☐ turbulence	[ˈtɜːbjələns]	*n.*	湍流
☐ jet lag			时差反应
☐ reschedule	[ˌriːˈʃedjuːl]	*v.*	重新安排时间
☐ guidebook	[ˈɡaɪdbʊk]	*n.*	旅行指南
☐ landmark	[ˈlændmɑːk]	*n.*	地标
☐ public transport			公共交通
☐ traffic congestion			交通堵塞
☐ pedestrian crossing			人行横道

Work & Business Vocabulary

These words frequently appear in office conversations, job interviews, and business presentations.

☐ career	[kəˈrɪə(r)]	*n.*	职业生涯
☐ occupation	[ˌɒkjʊˈpeɪʃ(ə)n]	*n.*	职业
☐ colleague	[ˈkɒliːɡ]	*n.*	同事
☐ employer	[ɪmˈplɔɪə(r)]	*n.*	雇主
☐ employee	[ɪmˈplɔɪiː]	*n.*	雇员
☐ freelancer	[ˈfriːlɑːnsə(r)]	*n.*	自由职业者
☐ internship	[ˈɪntɜːnʃɪp]	*n.*	实习
☐ vacancy	[ˈveɪkənsɪ]	*n.*	空缺职位
☐ recruitment	[rɪˈkruːtmənt]	*n.*	招聘
☐ interview	[ˈɪntəvjuː]	*n./v.*	面试
☐ résumé	[ˈrezjuːmeɪ]	*n.*	<美>简历
☐ salary	[ˈsælərɪ]	*n.*	工资
☐ bonus	[ˈbəʊnəs]	*n.*	奖金
☐ promotion	[prəˈməʊʃ(ə)n]	*n.*	晋升

☐ resign	[rɪˈzaɪn]	v. 辞职	
☐ retire	[rɪˈtaɪə(r)]	v. 退休	
☐ workload	[ˈwɜːkləʊd]	n. 工作量	
☐ deadline	[ˈdedlaɪn]	n. 截止日期	
☐ meeting	[ˈmiːtɪŋ]	n. 会议	
☐ conference	[ˈkɒnfərəns]	n. 会议，大型会谈	
☐ presentation	[ˌprez(ə)nˈteɪʃ(ə)n]	n. 演讲，展示	
☐ business trip		出差	
☐ negotiate	[nɪˈgəʊʃieɪt]	v. 谈判，协商	
☐ contract	[ˈkɒntrækt]	n. 合同	
☐ client	[ˈklaɪənt]	n. 客户	
☐ deal	[diːl]	n./v. 交易，协商	
☐ entrepreneur	[ˌɒntrəprəˈnɜː(r)]	n. 企业家	
☐ start-up	[stɑːtʌp]	n. 初创公司	
☐ merger	[ˈmɜːdʒə(r)]	n. 合并	
☐ investment	[ɪnˈvestmənt]	n. 投资	

Everyday Conversation & Social Situations Vocabulary

These words frequently appear in casual conversations, informal discussions, and social interactions.

☐ greeting	[ˈɡriːtɪŋ]	n. 问候
☐ introduce	[ˌɪntrəˈdjuːs]	v. 介绍
☐ invite	[ɪnˈvaɪt]	v. 邀请
☐ apologise	[əˈpɒlədʒaɪz]	v. 道歉
☐ request	[rɪˈkwest]	n./v. 请求
☐ complain	[kəmˈpleɪn]	v. 抱怨
☐ argue	[ˈɑːɡjuː]	v. 争论
☐ confirm	[kənˈfɜːm]	v. 确认
☐ refuse	[rɪˈfjuːz]	v. 拒绝
☐ agree	[əˈɡriː]	v. 同意
☐ persuade	[pəˈsweɪd]	v. 说服

☐ **recommend** [ˌrekəˈmend] *v.* 推荐

☐ **assure** [əˈʃʊə(r)] *v.* 确保，保证

☐ **chit-chat** [ˈtʃɪt tʃæt] *n.* 闲谈

☐ **catch up** 叙旧，更新信息

☐ **small talk** 闲聊

☐ **gossip** [ˈɡɒsɪp] *n./v.* 八卦，闲聊

☐ **interrupt** [ˌɪntəˈrʌpt] *v.* 打断

☐ **compliment** [ˈkɒmplɪmənt, *n./v.* 赞美
 ˈkɒmplɪment]

☐ **respond** [rɪˈspɒnd] *v.* 回应，回答

☐ **thankful** [ˈθæŋkfl] *adj.* 感激的

☐ **enthusiastic** [ɪnˌθjuːzɪˈæstɪk] *adj.* 热情的

☐ **awkward** [ˈɔːkwəd] *adj.* 尴尬的

☐ **sarcastic** [sɑːˈkæstɪk] *adj.* 讽刺的

Shopping & Consumerism Vocabulary

These words frequently appear in retail, e-commerce, and advertising-related listening tasks.

☐ **advertisement** [ədˈvɜːtɪsmənt] *n.* 广告

☐ **promotion** [prəˈməʊʃ(ə)n] *n.* 促销

☐ **discount** [ˈdɪskaʊnt, dɪsˈkaʊnt] *n.* 折扣 *v.* 打折

☐ **bargain** [ˈbɑːɡən] *n.* 便宜货

☐ **refund** [ˈriːfʌnd, rɪˈfʌnd] *n./v.* 退款

☐ **receipt** [rɪˈsiːt] *n.* 收据

☐ **exchange** [ɪksˈtʃeɪndʒ] *v./n.* 交换，换货

☐ **shopping mall** 购物中心

☐ **customer service** 客户服务

☐ **loyalty programme** 会员积分计划

☐ **consumer** [kənˈsjuːmə(r)] *n.* 消费者

☐ **impulse buying** 冲动消费

☐ **retailer** [ˈriːteɪlə(r)] *n.* 零售商

☐ **wholesale** [ˈhəʊlseɪl] *n.* 批发 *adj.* 批发的

☐ **e-commerce** [ˈiːkɒmərs] *n.* 电子商务

Weather & Natural Disasters Vocabulary

These words are common in weather forecasts, climate change discussions, and emergency warnings.

☐ forecast ['fɔ:kɑ:st] *n./v.* 预报

☐ temperature ['temprətʃə(r)] *n.* 温度

☐ humidity [hju:'mɪdətɪ] *n.* 湿度

☐ drought [draʊt] *n.* 干旱

☐ hurricane ['hʌrɪkən] *n.* 飓风

☐ tornado [tɔ:'neɪdəʊ] *n.* 龙卷风

☐ earthquake ['ɜ:θkweɪk] *n.* 地震

☐ tsunami [tsu:'nɑ:mɪ] *n.* 海啸

☐ flood [flʌd] *n.* 洪水

☐ avalanche ['ævəlɑ:nʃ] *n.* 雪崩

☐ landslide ['lændslaɪd] *n.* 山体滑坡

☐ climate change 气候变化

Entertainment & Arts Vocabulary

These words frequently appear in listening exercises related to movies, music, theatre, and literature.

☐ actor ['æktə(r)] *n.* 演员

☐ actress ['æktrəs] *n.* 女演员

☐ director [də'rektə(r)] *n.* 导演

☐ screenplay ['skri:npleɪ] *n.* 电影剧本

☐ script [skrɪpt] *n.* 剧本

☐ audience ['ɔ:dɪəns] *n.* 观众

☐ stage [steɪdʒ] *n.* 舞台

☐ performance [pə'fɔ:məns] *n.* 表演

☐ comedy ['kɒmədɪ] *n.* 喜剧

☐ drama ['drɑ:mə] *n.* 戏剧

☐ opera ['ɒprə] *n.* 歌剧

☐ rehearsal [rɪ'hɜ:s(ə)l] *n.* 排练

☐ orchestra ['ɔ:kɪstrə] *n.* 管弦乐队

☐ lyrics	['lɪrɪks]	n. 歌词
☐ exhibition	[ˌeksɪ'bɪʃ(ə)n]	n. 展览
☐ painting	['peɪntɪŋ]	n. 画作
☐ sculpture	['skʌlptʃə(r)]	n. 雕塑
☐ museum	[mjʊ'ziːəm]	n. 博物馆

Technology & Science Vocabulary

These words frequently appear in technology news, innovation discussions, and scientific reports.

☐ device	[dɪ'vaɪs]	n. 设备
☐ gadget	['gædʒɪt]	n. 小工具
☐ software	['sɒftweə(r)]	n. 软件
☐ hardware	['hɑːdweə(r)]	n. 硬件
☐ update	['ʌpdeɪt, ʌp'deɪt]	n./v. 更新
☐ download	[ˌdaʊn'ləʊd, 'daʊnləʊd]	v./n. 下载
☐ upload	[ʌp'ləʊd, 'ʌpləʊd]	v./n. 上传
☐ Wi-Fi	['waɪ faɪ]	n. 无线网络
☐ password	['pɑːswɜːd]	n. 密码
☐ robot	['rəʊbɒt]	n. 机器人
☐ laboratory	[lə'bɒrətri]	n. 实验室
☐ experiment	[ɪk'sperɪmənt]	n. 实验
☐ scientist	['saɪəntɪst]	n. 科学家
☐ microscope	['maɪkrəskəʊp]	n. 显微镜
☐ innovation	[ˌɪnə'veɪʃ(ə)n]	n. 创新

Environment & Sustainability Vocabulary

These words commonly appear in listening exercises related to global warming, pollution, and conservation.

☐ pollution	[pə'luːʃ(ə)n]	n. 污染
☐ global warming		全球变暖
☐ climate change		气候变化

☐ recycle	[ˌriːˈsaɪkl]	v. 回收利用
☐ waste	[weɪst]	n. 废物；浪费　v. 浪费
☐ renewable energy		可再生能源
☐ solar power		太阳能
☐ wind energy		风能
☐ biodiversity	[ˌbaɪəʊdaɪˈvɜːsəti]	n. 生物多样性
☐ deforestation	[ˌdiːˌfɒrɪˈsteɪʃn]	n. 森林砍伐
☐ plastic waste		塑料垃圾
☐ conservation	[ˌkɒnsəˈveɪʃ(ə)n]	n. 保护

Food & Nutrition Vocabulary

These words are useful for restaurant listening, diet discussions, and cooking programmes.

☐ meal	[miːl]	n. 餐
☐ ingredient	[ɪnˈɡriːdɪənt]	n. 配料
☐ recipe	[ˈresəpɪ]	n. 食谱
☐ cuisine	[kwɪˈziːn]	n. 菜系
☐ calories	[ˈkælərɪz]	n. 卡路里
☐ diet	[ˈdaɪət]	n. 饮食
☐ vegetarian	[ˌvedʒəˈteərɪən]	n. 素食主义者　adj. 素食的
☐ vegan	[ˈviːɡən]	n. 纯素食主义者
☐ junk food		垃圾食品
☐ fast food		快餐
☐ organic food		有机食品
☐ balanced diet		均衡饮食

Hobbies & Leisure Activities Vocabulary

These words frequently appear in conversations about free time and entertainment.

☐ hobby	[ˈhɒbɪ]	n. 爱好
☐ reading	[ˈriːdɪŋ]	n. 阅读
☐ writing	[ˈraɪtɪŋ]	n. 写作
☐ painting	[ˈpeɪntɪŋ]	n. 绘画

□ photography	[fə'tɒɡrəfɪ]	n. 摄影
□ gardening	['ɡɑ:dnɪŋ]	n. 园艺
□ knitting	['nɪtɪŋ]	n. 编织
□ woodworking	['wʊd,wɜ:kɪŋ]	n. 木工
□ camping	['kæmpɪŋ]	n. 露营
□ hiking	['haɪkɪŋ]	n. 徒步旅行
□ cycling	['saɪklɪŋ]	n. 骑自行车

Relationships & Family Vocabulary

These words are useful in listening tasks involving social interactions and family discussions.

□ family	['fæməlɪ]	n. 家庭
□ siblings	['sɪblɪŋz]	n. 兄弟姐妹
□ parents	['peərənts]	n. 父母
□ spouse	[spaʊs]	n. 配偶
□ marriage	['mærɪdʒ]	n. 婚姻
□ divorce	[dɪ'vɔ:s]	n./v. 离婚
□ friendship	['frendʃɪp]	n. 友谊
□ dating	['deɪtɪŋ]	n. 约会
□ engagement	[ɪn'ɡeɪdʒmənt]	n. 订婚

Public Transport & Traffic Vocabulary

These words are commonly heard in city navigation and commuting-related exercises.

□ bus stop		公交站
□ train station		火车站
□ platform	['plætfɔ:m]	n. 站台
□ subway	['sʌbweɪ]	n. 地铁
□ traffic jam		交通堵塞
□ pedestrian	[pɪ'destrɪən]	n. 行人
□ intersection	[,ɪntə'sekʃn]	n. 交叉路口

FCE LISTENING

FCE LISTENING

FCE LISTENING

FCE LISTENING

FCE LISTENING

FCE LISTENING

FCE LISTENING

FCE LISTENING

FCE LISTENING

Common Verbs & Their Paraphrases

- **buy**→purchase, acquire, get, obtain, make a transaction
- **sell**→trade, exchange, put up for sale, market
- **pay**→settle, cover the cost, make a payment
- **cancel**→call off, withdraw, revoke, terminate
- **increase**→rise, go up, climb, expand, escalate, boost
- **decrease**→drop, go down, fall, decline, shrink, reduce
- **improve**→enhance, upgrade, develop, refine, make better
- **fix**→repair, mend, restore, adjust, correct
- **decide**→determine, make up one's mind, conclude, settle on
- **explain**→clarify, elaborate, define, spell out
- **suggest**→recommend, propose, put forward, advise
- **change**→modify, alter, adjust, transform, revise
- **understand**→comprehend, grasp, make sense of, get
- **start**→begin, commence, initiate, set in motion
- **end**→finish, conclude, wrap up, bring to a close

Time-Related Words & Their Paraphrases

- **soon**→in a short time, before long, in the near future, shortly
- **immediately**→right away, at once, without delay, instantly
- **recently**→not long ago, a short while ago, in the past few days
- **before**→earlier, previously, prior to, ahead of time
- **after**→later, following, subsequently, afterward
- **forever**→permanently, indefinitely, for good
- **occasionally**→sometimes, from time to time, once in a while
- **frequently**→often, on a regular basis, repeatedly

Money & Finance-Related Words & Their Paraphrases

- **expensive**→costly, high-priced, overpriced, not cheap
- **cheap**→affordable, budget-friendly, low-cost, inexpensive
- **free**→complimentary, at no charge, provided at no cost
- **salary**→earnings, income, wages, paycheck
- **debt**→money owed, financial obligation, amount due
- **loan**→borrowed money, financial assistance, credit
- **refund**→money back, reimbursement, repayment

Work & Business-Related Words & Their Paraphrases

- **job**→occupation, profession, career, role, position

- colleague→coworker, workmate, teammate, associate
- boss→manager, supervisor, employer, executive
- company→business, firm, organisation, corporation
- workload→amount of work, job duties, tasks to complete
- promotion→career advancement, move up the ranks, higher position
- resign→quit, leave a job, step down
- fire→dismiss, let go, terminate, lose a job

Travel & Transportation-Related Words & Their Paraphrases

- trip→journey, travel, tour, excursion, getaway
- holiday→vacation, break, time off, leave
- flight→air travel, plane journey, trip by air
- arrive→reach, get to, come to, land
- depart→leave, set off, take off, begin the journey
- destination→final stop, travel location, place you're going to
- itinerary→travel plan, schedule, trip details
- baggage→luggage, suitcases, travel bags

Health & Medical-Related Words & Their Paraphrases

- sick→ill, unwell, not feeling well, under the weather
- recover→get better, heal, bounce back, regain health
- injury→wound, cut, bruise, sprain, damage
- medicine→treatment, drug, prescription, remedy
- hospital→medical centre, healthcare facility, clinic
- doctor→physician, medical expert, healthcare professional
- patient→someone receiving treatment, person under medical care

Everyday Conversation & Social Situations-Related Words & Their Paraphrases

- hello→hi, hey, good morning, greetings
- goodbye→see you later, take care, farewell, bye for now
- how are you→how's it going, how have you been, how's everything
- thank you→thanks, much appreciated, I'm grateful, cheers
- sorry→I apologise, my apologies, I regret that, excuse me
- excuse me→pardon me, may I have a moment, just a second

Entertainment & Arts-Related Words & Their Paraphrases

- movie→film, motion picture, cinema production
- music→song, melody, tune, composition
- theatre→stage play, drama performance, live show
- concert→live music event, show, performance

- **book**→novel, story, publication, literary work
- **painting**→artwork, portrait, canvas

Weather & Natural Disaster-Related Words & Their Paraphrases

- **rainy**→wet, drizzling, pouring, heavy showers
- **sunny**→bright, clear skies, warm weather
- **storm**→thunderstorm, bad weather, extreme conditions
- **flood**→high water levels, overflowing river, submerged area
- **earthquake**→ground shaking, seismic activity, tectonic movement

Environment & Sustainability-Related Words & Their Paraphrases

- **pollution**→environmental damage, contamination, waste problem
- **recycle**→reuse, process waste, make new from old
- **deforestation**→tree cutting, loss of forests, clearing land
- **global warming**→climate change, rising temperatures, environmental crisis
- **conserve**→protect, preserve, use efficiently

Public Transport & Traffic-Related Words & Their Paraphrases

- **bus**→public transport, coach, shuttle
- **train**→railway transport, metro, subway
- **taxi**→cab, private hire, ride service
- **traffic jam**→congestion, heavy traffic, roadblock
- **pedestrian**→walker, person on foot, foot traveller

Food & Nutrition-Related Words & Their Paraphrases

- **meal**→dish, food, plate
- **healthy**→nutritious, good for you, beneficial
- **junk food**→unhealthy snacks, processed food, fast food
- **organic food**→natural produce, chemical-free food
- **cooking**→preparing food, meal preparation, culinary activity

图书在版编目（CIP）数据

FCE听力从突破到跨越.II／王宏编著. --2版

北京：中国人民大学出版社，2025.6 --ISBN 978-7
-300-33909-2

Ⅰ.H319.9

中国国家版本馆CIP数据核字第2025JQ9486号

- 本书中所有理论、概念均系作者原创，如果引用需注明出处。
- 本书著作权归作者所有，出版权归中国人民大学出版社，任何复印、引用均需征求著作权人
  及出版权持有人同时同意。

FCE听力从突破到跨越（第二版）（II）

王宏　编著

FCE Tingli cong Tupo dao Kuayue (Di-er Ban) (II)

出版发行	中国人民大学出版社		
社　址	北京中关村大街31号	**邮政编码**	100080
电　话	010-62511242（总编室）	010-62511770（质管部）	
	010-82501766（邮购部）	010-62514148（门市部）	
	010-62511173（发行公司）	010-62515275（盗版举报）	
网　址	http://www.crup.com.cn		
经　销	新华书店		
印　刷	唐山玺诚印务有限公司		
开　本	787mm×1092mm　1/16	**版　次**	2021年1月第1版
			2025年6月第2版
印　张	7	**印　次**	2025年9月第2次印刷
字　数	80 000	**定　价**	39.80元（全两册）